10/22/74

DIVORCE

DIVORCE
What a woman needs to know

Barbara B. Hirsch

Henry Regnery Company, Chicago

Library of Congress Cataloging in Publication Data

Hirsch, Barbara B
 Divorce: what a woman needs to know.

 1. Divorce–United States. I. Title.
HQ834.H57   301.42'84'0973   72-11179

Published by Henry Regnery Company
114 West Illinois Street, Chicago, Illinois 60610
Manufactured in the United States of America
Library of Congress Catalog Card Number: 72-11179
International Standard Book Number: 0-8092-9109-6 (cloth)
            0-8092-9108-8 (paper)

To my father and mother

Contents

Foreword   ix

1 The Bonds of Matrimony   1
2 Annulment   4
3 Separate Maintenance   9
4 Divorce   12
5 Abandonment and Desertion   15
6 Adultery   25
7 Conviction of Crime   36
8 Gross Neglect of Duty   39
9 Habitual Drunkenness and Drug Addiction   42
10 Impotency   45
11 Insanity   50
12 Mental Cruelty   53
13 Physical Cruelty   59
14 Voluntary Separation   66
15 No Grounds—No-Fault   71
16 Defenses to Divorce   74

17 Your Lawyer and Your Lawyer's Fee   93
18 Where to Sue for Divorce   103
19 Child Custody   116
20 Visitation   124
21 The Child Support Allowance   129
22 Alimony   138
23 Income Tax   150
24 The Property Settlement Agreement   158
25 In Court   180
26 Post Decree—The Rest of Your Life   201
    *Chart—Grounds for Divorce Recognized in Each
        State*   216
    Index   219

Foreword

I could not write a book without formally dedicating it to my parents. Yet they will understand when I say that this book is a work dedicated also to the women who inspired it. Those women—the ones close to me, the ones who have spoken to me on a professional level, and those who have, in whispered, tremulous voices, asked "casual" questions at cocktail parties—led me to believe that a book explaining the legal ins and outs of divorce had to be written. I was and (even after months of struggling through sunshining Sundays trying to complete the manuscript) still am hopeful that this kind of book can answer some important questions for women contemplating divorce, in the throes of divorce, or rising out of the ashes of divorce.

I haven't attempted to explain why marriages fail, how to avoid emotional trauma, or how to readjust to the single life. Nor is this a do-it-yourself manual for divorce without lawyers. Domestic relations is an area that calls for professionals. A woman who proceeds to get a divorce without legal help is engaging in an activity that is nearly as dangerous as self-taught brain surgery.

I have attempted to describe, explain, and impart an understanding of the laws controlling dissolution of marriage, covering issues ranging from which courts have jurisdiction to which parent pays the orthodontist. What follows, then, is a study of the law with examples based on existing statutes or actual reported cases. Unlike most law books, however, this one isn't written for lawyers. And, unlike most treatises, this one is not designed to raise nice, theoretical controversy or ask intellectually stimulating questions.

This book is written for women, not *down* to women, but *to* women, and it is written to women who want and who need answers. I hope they will find them here.

BARBARA B. HIRSCH

1

The Bonds of Matrimony

THE preliminaries are dowsing in bubbly bath crystals, annointing in oils, depilating, and deodorizing. Then come the eye liners, mascaras, blushers, false eyelashes, lipsticks, face powders, hair coloring, and wigs, falls, and piles of Dynel curls. Wear a fiber-filled bra, adhere to the proper diet and exercise, and select a dress designed to catch his eye. Join church groups and study groups; walk a dog; frequent singles bars, singles cruises, and singles resorts; enroll in art classes, college classes and night classes. But, most of all, "Be your own sweet self."

You too can find a man. You too can buy a bridal gown, veil, stephanotis bouquet, engraved, deckle-edged invitations, champagne fountain, and dinner for 200. When all is said and done, the bride and groom will have launched their married life, entered a noble institution, commenced the business of reproducing the species, and joined the rush to the suburbs.

Once the vows are taken, the couple has acquired a new status, one that constitutes a distinct and different legal relationship to the state. One cannot convey a clear real estate title without the other; one cannot disinherit the other. Together they may file joint tax returns, incur debts on the other's credit, earn the other's Social Security benefits, and qualify for estate tax deductions. As long as they are married to each other, neither can marry someone else. And no matter how bitter the couple's disappointments, only death or dissolution in the courts can end this legal, married status and return them to the status of single persons.

* * *

Putting aside the "musts" prescribed by society-page editors and etiquette texts, and ignoring the tantrums of caterers and wedding consultants, the legal status of marriage may be achieved by applying to the state for a license, submitting to the necessary medical tests, and paying an authorized person to read the rites. This is ceremonial marriage and it is the acknowledged way of becoming husband and wife in every state. In most states you may even skip the license and the blood test without affecting the legal validity of the marriage (but you may have to spend your honeymoon in jail for violating the rules the state has laid down).

In about a dozen states, the legal status of marriage may be entered into without a license, without a blood test, and without a minister, rabbi, judge, sea captain, or any other third person making the pronouncement. These are the states that recognize the legality of common-law marriage. "Common-law wife" is the polite, veiled description employed by newspaper columnists to describe a movie actor's mistress, a gangster's moll, or any other woman who is openly shacking up. From a legal standpoint, the description is totally incorrect. A common-law wife is a legally married woman whose marriage was performed by a declaration between man and woman that they are husband and wife and whose behavior is consistent with that of married people. They are known as Mr. and Mrs., they file joint tax returns, they live together, and so forth. If they truly consider themselves married and live together as married in one of the states that recognizes marriage without "benefit of clergy," then they have the legal status of married people and only death or divorce can legally dissolve that status.

2

Annulment

Annulment is the legal procedure by which a judge declares a marriage null and void as if it had never existed. No matter how many bridesmaids and ushers, no matter how impressive the diamond wedding band, some "marriages" are not marriages at all. They are null and void and nothing can make them valid. A man and woman prohibited from marrying who have the ceremony anyway can have a dozen children and scores of grandchildren and still the "marriage" is not a marriage. At any moment, either spouse can up and leave. Since there's no legal status, there is nothing to dissolve.

What makes a marriage void and meaningless depends on the state that you call your home, but basically, void marriages are either incestuous or bigamous. The girl who devotes herself to finding a guy just like her daddy, pleases her mother, flatters her father, and gratifies Sigmund Freud. The young woman who settles down with her father is going to jail. Incest is sex between mother and son, father and daughter, grandparent and grandchild, brother and sister, and, depending on the state, uncles and nieces, aunts and nephews, and first cousins. A wedding between these relatives is no wedding at all, and it matters not that the couple intends a legitimate marriage, pays for the license, and hires a soprano to sing, "Oh, Promise Me." They are not married and even on their silver wedding anniversary the state will not recognize their married status.

A permissive outlook and liberal divorce laws now make it possible for a person to have a slew of spouses. But the only legal way to have them is one at a time. *Bigamy*, having two spouses, or *polygamy*, having three or more, are not only expensive and exhausting, they are criminal acts. The bigamist may not only go to jail, but any spouse after the first is not legally married. Again, the succeeding "marriages" are void from beginning to end.

Until only a few years ago, some states had "miscegenation" laws that said that interracial marriages were void, and that people entering into them could go to jail. The Supreme Court looked at these laws and at the Constitution and held that the choice to marry between races is a personal decision and not a legitimate concern of the state. Thus these laws are now out of date.

In general, the void marriages are the incestuous and bigamous ones. Ending these can be as simple as packing up and moving out, but if one is tidy and wants to clear up the legal records, the marriage can be declared void in a court annulment proceeding.

There are a flock of marriages that are "voidable." These are not automatically forbidden the way bigamous and incestuous marriages are. These are marriages where the bride and groom have a choice. Either they can live together and the marriage will be valid, or they can go to court and annul the marriage, making it void as if it had never existed.

For example, the high school freshman who marries the basketball forward may wake up to realize that marriage is more than cuddly weekends and that she can't even go to the sophomore dance at the gym because her husband can't afford an evening away from his job gassing cars at the car wash. She has the option of having her underage marriage annulled in a court or of staying married. Once she decides to stay on with her hero (and not give her folks the satisfaction of saying "I told you so."), and the first time she sleeps with her husband after the day she becomes "of age," she has confirmed the marriage and lost her chance for an annulment.

Despite all the pressures on girls to hurry up and get married, and with all the pressuring these girls put on their steady boyfriends, the law still is that a marriage entered into under duress may be voided by annulment. Duress, though, is not the impatient prodding of the bride's mother, but rather the more direct and threatening insistence of her shotgun-toting father. A groom (or bride) forced to the altar by that kind of menace can march directly from the church to the courthouse and annul the marriage. If, though, he stops along the way to enjoy his wedding night, he has ratified the marriage and has lost the right to annul it.

The bride and groom must really intend to get married. A boy tripping on LSD, who decides to marry the nearest female and actually finds a preacher and goes through with it, can annul as soon as he is conscious of what he has done. A group of Ivy Leaguers was driving through New England, picnicking and generally having a good time when two of them decided to get married for the fun of it. They stopped at a justice of the peace, giggled through the ceremony, said "I do," and then, realizing what they had done, sought to annul the marriage. The high court of Connecticut held that they never intended to marry, and as they never had the "honeymoon," the marriage was annulled.

Another reason for annulment of a marriage is fraud. As any freshman law student can tell you, fraud is: "He lied; he intended to lie; you relied on his lie; you were injured thereby." Yet, heaven knows, there's a little bit of fraud in every courtship. You never let him see you with rollers in your hair and cold cream on your face; he promised you a trip to Europe, a membership in the country club, and a full-time maid. And it's a relief for the multitudes to know that pretending to be a virgin is not fraud sufficient for annulment. Fortunately for the institution of marriage, these wee misrepresentations don't amount to fraud for the purpose of annulment. In order for an annulment to be granted because of fraud, the injured party must show that the other's lie went right to the essence of the marriage relationship.

For example, if he forgot to mention that he was impotent, that's fraud.* A blushing bride who is just a little pregnant by another man may be guilty of fraud. One young man married the chaste flower of his dreams; only three days after the ceremony, however, she gave birth to a robust baby boy. That's fraud. Another woman gave birth eight months after the wedding, but the judge refused to annul the marriage because "there was not sufficient evidence that she was pregnant when she married him." The man who has intercourse with his girlfriend, marries her, and soon finds himself a father is seldom granted an annulment. The courts don't want to punish a man for playing around, but they are very reluctant to declare a baby a bastard.

All *voidable* marriages (as opposed to bigamous and incestuous marriages, which are absolutely *void*) can be dissolved only by court proceedings. The wronged person must go to court to *avoid* the marriage, and the judge must annul it or the marriage will be valid. Then too, *voidable*

---

*Impotency as a ground for annulment is the same as impotency as a ground for divorce. See chapter ten.

marriages may be ratified, or confirmed, and no annulment will be allowed. For example, if a couple who marries for a lark goes on a honeymoon, they have ratified and the marriage is valid; if a man whose wife delivers a bouncing five-month term babe climbs back into bed with her, he's accepted the marriage and can't annul later. So, while no amount of sexual intercourse will make a *void* marriage valid, one occasion of sexual intercourse, after full knowledge of the facts, will make a *voidable* marriage valid.

3

Separate Maintenance

MARRIAGE, according to the poets and lyricists, is a bundle of joy. It is, according to the law, a bundle of rights and obligations. In most states, for example, a wife is her husband's agent. Thus when she buys the groceries, clothing for herself and the children, furniture for the house, and otherwise incurs family expenses normal to her family's standard of living, she may charge them to her husband's account. The store that sells these family expense items may collect from the wife or the husband. The dentist who treats the wife and children may send his bill either to the husband or the wife. The married couple who have children have a legal duty to feed, clothe, shelter, and educate them, and the doctor who stitches a child's head after a playground accident may turn to the patient's daddy to collect.

Now what happens if one day, the husband-father-bread-winner gets tired of his usual routine. He rents an apartment in a swinging singles hi-rise and leaves suburbia. On the way to his new life, our hero stops at the shopping center and tells all of the store credit managers that his wife is no longer to charge things to his credit. From now on, he "will be responsible for his debts only." The stores, being careful to extricate themselves from a domestic quarrel, and fearing that the worst may happen, that a bill may go uncollected, promptly show their loyalty to the woman who has made purchases in their stores. They cancel her charge account; they insist that she pay cash on the line.

Can a man simply ignore his responsibilities to his wife and children when he decides to think only of himself? Certainly not. The abandoned housewife can file for divorce; she can get alimony; she can get child support—and she'll get divorced, too.

For some women, divorce isn't the answer. Some women will patiently await their husband's return from his flight of fancy. When he decides to come home, they'll welcome him. Other women will not divorce because of the teachings of their religion. Still others, particularly older and more practical women, would rather stay married and wait around for insurance policies, Social Security, pension fund, death benefits, and the other goodies that will come their way when their husband's escapades catch up with them, and these devoted wives are rendered widows.

Whatever the reason, a married woman may stay married. Assuming that her husband has no grounds to divorce her, she may do nothing and remain the wandering husband's wife. But what happens if her "bachelor-husband" closes her charge accounts, forgets to make the mortgage payments, and doesn't bother to mail her an allowance to care for her and the children? She may sue him for separate maintenance.

Separate maintenance is the court's order requiring an errant husband to maintain his wife and family while they are living apart. Separate maintenance is sometimes called "divorce from bed and board," but it is not a divorce from the bonds of matrimony. In fact, it is neither an order of divorce nor annulment. The marriage is intact and remains so, and the spouses can reunite at any time. The property is not divided up; neither party can claim sole ownership of the house and neither can ask the judge to declare him sole owner of the household furnishings. The law does no more than assure that the husband will dispense his duty to support his family.

4

Divorce

I⊤ would be crass (and pessimistic) to suggest
that the marriage service be amended to read, "Til death,
or divorce, do us part." In fact, though, there are *two* ways
a valid marriage can end. One is death, the other is divorce.

Divorce is a legal proceeding to end a legal relationship.
There are three parties to every marriage: the husband, the
wife, and the state. Likewise, there must be three parties to
every divorce: the husband, the wife, and the state. No matter
how progressive the couple, no matter how permissive the
state, divorce cannot be agreed upon between the spouses
without the state taking a hand in it. A couple can live apart
for years. He may have abandoned her at Niagara Falls.
They may have a mutual hatred or a total disregard for each
other. If they are Catholics, the Pope may have nullified the
marriage under canon law. If they are Jewish, they may
obtain a "get," a religious divorce. But so far as the state

is concerned, this unloving couple is husband and wife and only a divorce proceeding in its court and a divorce decree signed by its judge will mean that the bonds of matrimony are legally dissolved.

Divorce is the state's act to restore husband and wife to the status of single people. Divorce proceedings fix the care, support, and visitation of the spouses' offspring. Divorce divides up the family wealth. Divorce makes it possible for each to marry again. The right and the power to do all of these things is in the state and it is only the state that may declare when and how a marriage becomes an un-marriage.

It may seem presumptuous, nervy, and nosey for the legislators to sit down in the assembly hall in your state capitol and decide the terms under which you are entitled to divorce your husband. Yet that is exactly what happens.

A state assemblyman introduces a bill. The bill then goes to committee. The committee ponders, discusses, and holds hearings. The bill is reported to the assembly as a whole. The assembly votes and it is decided that if he beats you up, skips town, embarrasses you, intimidates you, ignores you, or sleeps with his best friend's wife, you have legal reason to seek a divorce in the courts of the state in which you live.

Grounds for divorce are the reasons that the state legislators think justify a suit to dissolve your marriage. Up until a few years ago, the legislators in New York declared that the only legal reason to dissolve a marriage was adultery. No other reason would do and the courts of the state of New York could dissolve no marriage without proof of adultery.

The first step to divorce then is not the first step down the wedding aisle. The first step is the first time that the husband (or wife) conducted himself in a way that the state declares as justifying its court in granting a divorce. State laws vary, of course, but most states agree that divorces may be granted on the grounds of mental or physical cruelty, adultery, abandonment, drunkenness, drug addiction, impotency, and insanity, among others.* The following chapters explain these grounds, what they mean, and how they are proven.

---

*The chart at the back of the book gives the grounds for divorce recognized in each state.

5

Abandonment and Desertion

SHIRTS piled high on the bed, dresser drawers pulled open, golf clubs dragged up from the basement, the suitcase lid closed, wham, the front door shut, slam. He's gone and the house is silent. Every day the divorce court judges hear this tale.

He left you: that's desertion and abandonment. What could be simpler? A lot. Five questions must be answered according to the law before a divorce will be granted for abandonment and desertion.

1. Did he intend to desert you?
2. Did you consent to his desertion?
3. Did the desertion continue for the period of time required by your state legislature?
4. Has the marriage relationship ended?
5. Did you behave so badly that he was within his rights in leaving you?

15

1. Did he intend to desert you?—Desertion and abandonment must be willful, and as the Florida statute says, the desertion must be obstinate. He has to have made up his mind to leave you.

Most deserting husbands announce their plans to move in with their girl friends, or become half of an "odd couple" with one of their Thursday night card-playing buddies. Some men will leave you a sweet note telling you to see a divorce lawyer; others will leave in a cacophony of slammed doors and roaring engines. All of these actions make it clear that they "intend to desert" and that their abandonment is "willful and obstinate."

There are a few cases, though, where women have been left alone and their spouses didn't intend to desert. One bridegroom returned from his honeymoon to find Uncle Sam waiting to take him on an all-expense-paid tour of Southeast Asia. His being drafted into the army constituted a separation, but there was no intention on his part to abandon his bride. Distraught Alabama parents locked their daughter in the house when they learned of her marriage; she was separated, but she didn't intend to desert her husband. Did Ronald Coleman intend to abandon Greer Garson in *Random Harvest*? Not on your life; a simple case of amnesia, you know. Is a bank robber's "get-away" an intentional desertion of his wife? Is a pickpocket's year in jail a willful and obstinate desertion of his family? No, unless you are from North Carolina, or a state with a similar statute on desertion, men separated because of criminal acts have not voluntarily intended to desert and abandon their wives.

While it's fair to say that your spouse is probably not an amnesia victim or a fugitive, another category of unintentional deserters is becoming more and more commonplace. This man is known as the Corporate Executive. Here's how it usually happens. A sorority queen marries the man mostly likely to succeed. As time goes on, he graduates from corporate trainee to assistant to the assistant. While he's going from Brooks Brothers gray flannel to custom-tailored pinstripe, she's furnishing an ultramodern bi-level in charming antiques. The suburb is bright and clean, the children are teachers' pets and are busy with extracurricular activities. One day, our hero comes home with the big news. He's been promoted to vice-president in charge of regional sales. He announces that he has a big raise, a big bonus, a brand-new region, and —"We're all moving to Lonely Cactus, Montana." The wife says "No," the kids say "No," and off he goes without them. Is he a deserter? No. It is the husband, the man (the male chauvinist, if you see it that way), who has the right to choose the domicile for his wife and children and they must follow.

When it discussed this subject, the Supreme Court of Georgia went so far as to declare, as a matter of law, that "In this state, the husband is the head of the family. . . ." So, when our Corporate Executive goes off to pursue new heights on the sales charts, he is *not* an intentional, willful, or obstinate deserter. On the contrary, the *wife* who refuses to follow her husband is deserting and abandoning him, and *she* will be guilty of this ground for divorce. Unless the woman is the breadwinner and the husband is the homemaker, or until the women's rights movement brings about its revolution, the husband chooses the domicile and the wife must follow or be chargeable with desertion and abandonment.

There is, fortunately, one exception to the wife's absolute duty to follow her husband. When the husband's choice of domicile is unsafe or unsuitable, she need not go with him, and if he actually does go without her, he will be held to have deserted his wife. For example, an asthmatic, allergic wife need not leave Arizona for Los Angeles. Indeed, the law displays genuine compassion when it declares that so long as he is financially able to provide a home, he cannot require his wife to move into a hostile household with his parents.

The New Jersey chancery court dramatically made the point that a woman is entitled to be in charge of her own home when it said that a wife "is entitled to a home in which she alone is mistress. It may, of necessity, be nothing more than a hovel on the edge of a swamp and she is duty-bound to go there, but it is her privilege to be mistress thereof."

One man lost his suit for divorce when he claimed that his wife deserted and abandoned him by refusing to live with him in his parents' house. The judge held that the wife was fully within her rights and denied his divorce. The judge had learned that the wife was treated with habitual and unconcealed contempt by her in-laws. Her mother-in-law was so determined to break up the marriage that she put the young couple in a bedroom shared with a fourteen-year-old boy boarder. A man simply cannot confront his wife with the decision of living unhappily with him and his parents or living apart from him. If he does, *he* is deserting his wife and not vice versa.

2. Did you consent to his desertion?—For a spouse to be guilty of abandonment and desertion, obviously he must abandon and desert—that is, he must walk out on you, take himself out of your life. If you've agreed that it would be best if the two of you lived apart, he's not guilty of deserting you.

3. Did the desertion continue for the period of time required by your state legislature?—Some married men punctuate every spat with a weekend away. Some women go "home" hoping that their absence will make their husbands' hearts grow fonder. Desertion is grounds for divorce, only if one's leaving was for the purpose of leaving and not for the purpose of ending an argument or making a point.

The state laws on desertion and abandonment require that the desertion be continuous for an extended period of time, generally six months to three years, depending on where you're from and how strongly against divorce your legislature is. The desertion and abandonment must continue without interruption, and without resumption of the marital relationship, during the entire period specified.

It is easy to compute the time he's been gone and figure out if it's long enough to meet the requirements of the statute. However, sometimes the arithmetic is complicated by a separate maintenance proceeding. When separate maintenance was discussed, it was said that the judges do not order the husband and wife to live apart. Separate maintenance simply provides that a wife already living apart from her husband may apply to the court for an order requiring him to support her. Separate maintenance doesn't *cause* desertion and abandonment. The spouse must have deserted *before* a separate maintenance allowance can be sought.

The legislators in most states understand the nature of separate maintenance and they realize that if a man deserts and refuses to provide support for his wife and children, she might be destitute and forced to seek a separate maintenance allowance from him during the time he's gone. In most states the time during which a separate maintenance suit was pending and during which the husband pays a separate maintenance allowance is *not* deducted from the time period required for a suit for desertion.

Here's how it works. A Skokie, Illinois man, lured by what he thought was the swinging singles life on Rush Street in Chicago, left his wife. He declared his independence on July 4, 1971. He moved into a "pad" fitted out with plastic dinnerware and furnished in the style of a sleazy motel. As the summer passed, he conveniently forgot to provide for his family. In September, his wife sued for separate maintenance, and the court ordered our aging hipster to make a weekly support payment to her. As the months passed, the Skokie expatriate became disenchanted with TV dinners and found he was not making it with the stewardesses of his dreams. Yet he showed no signs of returning. By July 4, 1972, he'd been gone for the year required by Illinois law. There's no deduction for the period of separate maintenance, and his Skokie wife may obtain her divorce decree for his desertion and abandonment.

The timer on desertion starts when the door slams and continues nonstop until you get a divorce *or* until he returns. If your state calls for willful desertion for three years, for example, and he leaves for two years, he is allowed to have a change of heart and to ask to come home. The time period stops from the day he makes a good-faith offer of reconciliation. Even if you turn him down and he's gone another year, this constitutes only two years of desertion, not the three required by your state. In fact, if you refuse to accept his good-faith offer of reconciliation, from the day you refuse him, *you* are the deserter and after three years, he may divorce you.

If your spouse is guilty of other grounds of divorce, either before or during his absence, you need not take him back. You can go right ahead and get your divorce on grounds of mental cruelty, or physical cruelty, or adultery, or whatever else he is guilty of. Note, too, that in order to stop the desertion timer from running, the offer of reconciliation must be *in good faith*. If the deserter's "change of heart" comes because his lawyer tells him he's going to get caught for a fistful of alimony, his offer of reconciliation may be only to deprive you of your grounds for divorce and is *not* in good faith. You can refuse him without forfeiting your right to sue him for desertion. Unless you want him back and are willing to accept his offer to come home, you should tell him you have to think about it and let your lawyer help you make up your mind.

4. Has the marriage relationship ended?—Marriage can end legally only by death or divorce. In order that a divorce be granted for abandonment and desertion, though, the judge must be convinced that the marriage *relationship* has ended. The marriage relationship is the personal, emotional alliance between husband and wife. If this has become known as "togetherness," then abandonment and desertion are marked by "apartness." The law often describes the end of the marriage relationship as "separation from bed and board." That is, you take up separate addresses and separate lives. If he stops in for an occasional weekend visit and you share the same bed, you haven't ended the marriage relationship.

Not only must you occupy separate beds, you also should be eating your meals apart, that is, at a separate "board" or dining table. But, unlike occasional sex, an occasional meal together is allowable. For example, let's imagine that your state says the marriage relationship must cease for a year. He walks out on New Year's Day, 1972, and moves into his own apartment (or freeloads at his folks' house). If he takes you out to dinner now and then during 1972, the law still considers the marriage relationship ended (if he spends the night with you, you are resuming the marriage relationship and he's yours to keep).

So long as you are separated, he can (and should) support you and the children and visit them during that year. His sending you checks, paying your bills, and seeing his children does not resume the marriage relationship. He is still a deserter. He is merely performing a legal duty, not resuming the personal marital relationship.

While most states' laws require that you and your husband actually take up separate residences in order to "end the marriage relationship," a few states recognize that even a couple living under the same roof can be miles apart. One judge said that in determining the end of the marriage relationship, "the essential thing is not separate roofs, but separate lives." A man won a divorce when he claimed that his wife deserted him although they lived in the same house. She totally ignored him, cooked her own meals and ate them alone, refused to join him socially, and utterly refused to have sexual relations with him. She testified, in fact, that rather than sleep with him, she'd prefer to "have her throat cut from ear to ear." The judge saw all of this conduct as the end of the marriage relationship. Remember, though, that this is the exception. In most states, there can be no desertion without an actual separation, the taking up of separate residences.

5. *Did you behave so badly that he was within his rights in leaving you?*—A husband, or wife, will not be guilty of desertion if life was so miserable at home that he or she was justified in leaving. As a general rule, in order to entitle a spouse to leave home, the other spouse must have been guilty of behavior that is serious enough to be grounds for divorce. When Mrs. S went home to mama and stayed there, Mr. S sued her for divorce claiming she had abandoned him. The judge denied the divorce and said Mrs. S was perfectly within her rights in moving out, especially since she did so the day Mr. S punched her, breaking her teeth. One lady was found to be innocent of desertion when she testified that the day before she left, her husband had hit her, knocked her down, carried her off, and tied her to a cot in the basement. Keeping his promise to the children, he then went off with them for a day of swimming at the "Y." When they returned home, he had sexual intercourse with his wife, and *then* untied her. Certainly, she was justified in removing herself from him.

What if the lady has no place to go, or decides that she is entitled to stay right there in her own house and that her husband should be the one to leave? We've come to one of the questions women with domestic problems most often ask: "Can I lock him out?"

A deserter is a person who removes himself from the marital relationship. Almost always, then, the deserter is the one who *leaves* home. But there is also the deserter who never walks out, who stays at the homestead and yet is still guilty in law of deserting and abandoning his spouse. Such a spouse is guilty of what the law calls "constructive" desertion and abandonment. We've already seen three examples of this. The first is the wife who refuses to follow her husband to a suitable new domicile chosen by him. Remember the Corporate Executive? The second is the spouse who will have nothing to do with his mate though they stay under the same roof. The third example is the wife who refuses the spouse's good-faith offer of reconciliation and won't allow him to come home.

There is another situation where one puts her mate away from her and is therefore guilty of desertion even without moving out. This is the wife who, without justification, locks the spouse out of the marital home. This is the way it goes. Mr. O wakes up one morning in a horrible mood. He makes his way to the kitchen for his breakfast. Mrs. O is bustling about frying bacon, scrambling eggs, and baking biscuits. He grunts his "good morning," opens the newspaper, and starts reading while shoveling food into his mouth. All is quiet until he gets to her coffee. "You just can't make good coffee," he shouts, jumps up, and goes off to work. Mrs. O is furious. As soon as the car clears the driveway, she's calling the locksmith to change all the locks. At dinnertime, Mr. O returns home from work having forgotten completely about the "coffee episode." He puts his car in the garage and comes around to the back door, as usual. His key doesn't fit in the lock. He rings the bell, he bangs on the screens: no response. He goes to the front door. There, on the steps, he finds his suitcases packed and waiting for him. He takes the bags and checks into a hotel. Now, if Mrs. O should keep this up for the statutory time period, she has deserted and abandoned her husband, and she's never left the marital home. Clearly, Mrs. O has excessive pride in her coffee and a terrible temper.

For constructive desertion with a vengeance though, she's

no match for one Midwestern wife. She swore to false evidence regarding her husband's sanity and had him forcibly removed from the house and confined to a mental institution. It took complex court proceedings to establish his competence and restore his freedom, which he exercised by promptly returning to court and divorcing the little woman.

Locking out your spouse may then be desertion on your part, *unless* you are justified. Justification is generally found when your spouse has himself been guilty of grounds for divorce. You are entitled to change the locks, for example, when your physical safety is threatened. A woman may protect herself by leaving home or locking out a dangerous or threatening husband without being guilty of desertion. Remember, too, that your lawyer may, in most states, seek an injunction whereby the court will order that such a spouse move out of the house and leave you in peace.

Whether a spouse is justified in locking out his mate then raises the legal issue of his guilt of other grounds for divorce, so before you call the locksmith, be sure you call your lawyer.

6

Adultery

THE divorce law does not demand that you remember the Sabbath and keep it holy. It doesn't care if you covet thy neighbor's wife or his manservant or his ass. You need not love thy neighbor as thyself. But *thou shalt not commit adultery*! Every state has different divorce laws, but in every state adultery is grounds for divorce.

As any woman's lib advocate will tell you, in early history adultery had a definition made by men and for men. Adultery was committed *only* when a married woman had sexual intercourse with a man who was not her husband. A married man could cheat freely: adultery didn't apply to him. And it should be no surprise to the civil libertarians of both sexes that when adultery was finally applied to both men and women, there were several court cases questioning whether a man could be guilty of committing adultery with a female slave. She was, after all, her master's property—couldn't he do with his property as he pleased? No, the law said. A man

25

could be guilty of adultery for loving his neighbor's wife as his own or for loving his servant.

Adultery is the voluntary sexual intercourse of a married person with a person other than his spouse. Note: adultery is *voluntary* sexual intercourse. If a married woman is raped, her husband, the sweet, understanding man that he is, cannot divorce her on the grounds of adultery. On the other hand, when J, a sensuous man, raped a fourteen-year-old schoolgirl, Mrs. J was within her rights in divorcing him.

Remember, too, that adultery is voluntary *sexual intercourse*. Kissing, hugging, general cuddling, and your standard petting are *not* adultery. Only fornication qualifies. One day, Mr. W had a terrible head cold and took an early train home from the office. He immediately forgot his sniffles when he strolled into his bi-level and found Mrs. W, naked, entertaining a gentleman caller. Mr. W grabbed some nasal spray and headed straight back to the city to see his lawyer. When he sued his wife on the grounds of adultery, Mrs. W called her doctor to the witness stand. He testified that because of a serious illness and surgery, Mrs. W had an abnormal vagina and that "not the slightest degree of penetration was possible." True, said Mr. W but what about fellatio? I saw her doing that. No go. Fellatio is *not* sexual intercourse, and therefore Mrs. W was *not* guilty of adultery.

Mr. W might have won a divorce had he sued on the grounds of mental cruelty, but poor Mrs. N. Y. had no such choice. Until the mid-1960s, the *only* ground for divorce in the state of New York was adultery. When Mrs. N. Y., in 1951, proved beyond a reasonable doubt that her husband had committed cunnilingus with another woman, she had not proven adultery and she did not get her divorce.

Probably out of deference to Mrs. N. Y.'s plight, when the legislature in Albany finally revised the New York divorce law, it defined adultery specifically as sexual intercourse and also "deviate sexual conduct" including fellatio and cunnilingus. Virginia allows divorce for "adultery, or sodomy, or buggery,"* and North Carolina grounds include "unnatural or abnormal sex act with a person of the same sex or of a different sex or with a beast." In general, though, adultery is plain, uncluttered sexual intercourse.

Proving Adultery

No matter how overwhelming the passion, no matter how grand the amour, adultery rarely is performed in broad daylight in the presence of witnesses. It is difficult to catch your spouse, as the lawyers say, in *flagrante delicto*, in the flagrant wrong. This is not to say that it doesn't happen. Knowing that Mrs. S didn't share his enthusiasm for golf, Mr. S simply arranged to meet his girl friend at the golf range every evening. There they hit out a couple of buckets of balls, hugged, kissed, and retired to the backseat of his automobile. Mrs. S became suspicious of her husband's devotion to the sport, so she arranged with several of her friends to follow him. They watched the couple slicing and hooking and then easing their way to the parking lot. They waited and then came up to the parked car, and in the light of two large spotlights saw the husband "getting off the defendant. His pants were open and her dress was up." Mrs. S shouted, "you've been committing adultery." Mr. S looked up and with the poise of Arnold Palmer stroking his final putt at the Masters said, "What of it?"

Another man showed far less presence of mind. When his wife and her witnesses burst into the room, he and his mistress tried to hide under the bed. At the stroke of midnight, Mrs. Cuckold left the revelers in her neighbor's living room to find her husband and give him a New Year's Eve kiss. She located him in the basement recreation room in the act of sexual intercourse. She called to the lovers to stop, and

---

* "Buggery" is sexual intercourse between a human being and an animal.

they did stop—after her second request. Hurriedly, she took her husband home. The next day, she and her husband returned to their hosts: (1) to thank them for a lovely evening, (2) to apologize, and (3) to retrieve his underwear. Wives have discovered their husbands with girl friends in bedrooms and hotel rooms, and one unfaithful spouse was surprised in the act of intercourse in the serenity of the local cemetery.

It takes a truly indiscreet spouse to be caught in the act —so adultery, like all the best mysteries, is most often proved by circumstantial evidence.

However, in order to prove adultery without having detectives bursting into a motel room with flashbulbs popping, you must rely on more than your mah-jongg club's gossip. You must prove that your spouse and his alleged sweetheart had an adulterous disposition and that they had an opportunity to commit the act. Boiled down, that means that you must be able to prove the time, place, opportunity, and disposition to commit adultery. You should be able to provide your lawyer with the approximate date of the liaison and the place where it happened. You should prove that he and the other woman were alone together for enough time, and that they were sufficiently interested in each other sexually that they would have made use of that time and place to have sexual intercourse.

If time, place, and opportunity seem simple enough, but disposition to commit adultery sounds a little involved, an example may help. Mr. N and Miss M meet at a secluded retreat. They disappear into a room alone together for several hours. They emerge from the room, holding hands and smiling at each other. Photographers are waiting outside—cameras click, reporters take notes. If Mr. N is Joe Nasty and Miss M is Mona Mammary, his mini-skirted, swivel-hipped secretary who received a mink stole, you may have a case. But if Mr. N is Richard Nixon and Miss M is Golda Meir, who received a Phantom jet plane, forget it. These are chiefs of state having a private meeting, and while I'm not implying that the President and the Israeli chief of state are asexual, it's fair, I think, to say that the disposition to commit adultery just wouldn't be present.

Mr. B admitted that he and a female companion spent long hours alone together but denied that they were disposed to commit adultery. He argued that he was writing his memoirs and Mrs. X was doing the typing. But he was found guilty when he was unable to produce even a page of the manuscript. Mr. D, on the other hand, told the judge that although he visited a brothel, he never did more than play the madam's piano. But there was no piano at "The Palace," and Mr. D was found guilty of committing adultery with his hometown's infamous prostitute, Miss Myrtle.

Even though the chicken coop was said to be fitted out with bedroom furnishings, Mr. A was unable to convince the judge that his wife's frequent visits there were for anything but tending to the hens.

Once you have evidence of the time, the place, and the opportunity, the judge may find adulterous disposition from evidence of public displays of affection like hand-holding. The giving and receiving of personal gifts also has served to prove adulterous disposition. When Mr. O escorted a woman on her vacation, paid her expenses, and shared her hotel room, the judge thought it fair to assume that she showed her gratitude with "slightly more than kisses." A divorce was granted to the wife whose husband received both his paramour's lingerie and her communicable disease.

Proving adultery, though, is extremely difficult, even in Kentucky, where men are given the edge. There a man is allowed to prove a charge of adultery against his wife, if she engages in "such lewd or lascivious behavior . . . as proves her to be unchaste" even without proof of adultery.

If you're reading this chapter with more than casual interest, I'll bet your husband has telephoned to tell you that he's working late again. And I'll bet, too, that you called the office an hour later and the phone rang and rang Perhaps your "best friend" ran into your husband dining with a voluptuous "client" and couldn't wait to report it to you. But suspicions and gossip are not proof, and indiscretion is not adultery. What the lawyers call "hard evidence" is not easy to obtain. An Arizona woman took movies of her husband and his mistress. A Midwestern woman and her lady friends checked into a hotel room armed with stethoscopes to testify to a highly personal conversation going on in the room next door. Mrs. C hired a handwriting expert to testify that a motel registration of "Mr. and Mrs. John Smith" was actually in Mr. C's penmanship. The birth of a child to a woman whose army husband had been in Southeast Asia is another example of "hard evidence."

Occasionally a guilty spouse will admit his peccadilloes in court. A septuagenarian could hardly contain his pride when admitting to his sexual escapades—which included an affair with his daughter-in-law. Judges, though, are wary of trumped-up divorces and often will disbelieve the defendant's voluntary admissions.*

Then there's the willing testimony of the alleged paramour—another witness who is rarely believed. Surely you've heard the stories of the fraternity of man, particularly the one where the pregnant girl accuses her "steady" of being the father of her child and his fraternity brothers rise to his defense by fervently swearing that they all had intercourse with her. In a recent paternity case, a judge was so disgusted by the obvious lies told by the boy's basketball teammates that he threatened to have them all share in the child's support. Divorce court judges are equally aware of the possibility that a man may rise to his buddy's aid by the simple act of dishonoring his wife and perjuring himself.

---

* See chapter sixteen, which deals with the defense of collusion.

In a recent Nebraska case, the judge totally discounted the testimony of a man who brazenly set out to destroy the reputation of a woman he was supposed to have loved, leaving the witness stand, in the judge's words, "as a gigolo and self-appointed cad." But notice that I've referred to the admissions of both the defendant-spouse and the lover as "willing" and "voluntary." The reluctant yet sincere admission coming as a result of vigorous cross-examination will be believed.

Judges are most reluctant to accept the testimony of the divorcing couple's child and rarely will rely on that testimony. A toddler may give a stirring, but totally misleading, account of having seen mommy kissing Santa Claus. And even a hair-raisingly detailed report of just what daddy did when momma was away getting baby brother is often discounted. First, children have super imaginations and an acute ability to seek revenge against one parent in order to get attention from the other. Second, the judges have decided that it's not wise to encourage children to spy on their parents. Third, a parent should be reluctant to put even his teen-age child into the middle of a divorce suit.

If your husband is out again and you're home alone watching one of television's private eye shows or reading a Mike Hammer episode, you've undoubtedly considered hiring a detective. Most cities will list investigators and detective agencies in the Yellow Pages. Many of them specialize in "domestic" work and photography, and some advertise that they might "alleviate your suspicions."

A detective agency hired to follow someone for one day in a large city normally will assign two men and a car to the job. They will "tail" your husband and then prepare a typewritten report. The rates vary, but you can expect to spend about $80.00 for each eight-hour day and there probably will be an extra charge for photographs and witness fees for the detectives' in-court testimony. Undoubtedly, there are many reputable, honest, and skilled professionals engaged in detective work, but there are also a few bad apples. There is, for example, the unscrupulous detective who will confront your husband with a damaging report on his behavior and turn it over to him for a price. Then there are investigators who just can't seem to do anything right.

Mrs. B hired a team of detectives to watch her husband. They laid elaborate plans to catch him in the act, following him for several days and reporting his activities. Then one day, Mr. B was seen entering the home of his suspected sweetheart. Carefully, the detectives loaded their cameras; quietly, they waited at the door. After a half hour, they burst into the room—to find Mr. B sitting with the "other woman." Both were fully dressed; both were drinking coffee at the kitchen table. The photographs, which look lovely in the family album, were worthless as evidence of adultery.

Mrs. J's detectives did a somewhat better job. They testified to seeing Mr. J lying down in the back of a car with the co-respondent, but his "trousers were up" and his coat was on. They couldn't remember if the co-respondent was wearing her glasses or whether her slacks were on or off, open or closed. The judge reminded them that indiscretion is not adultery and held the testimony insufficient to prove that sexual intercourse had occurred.

The court's policy is to accept the testimony of hired investigators, but to scrutinize it with great care. A detective, like anyone else, wants to have a job well done and if you hire him to find your husband in an awkward situation, he may, in his zeal to perform his task, see even the mundane as the awkward. Then there's the added risk that your husband may be loving and faithful to you. If he learns that you have hired someone to spy on him, don't expect him to be understanding. The use of private detectives is always a last resort—not a first choice.

Naming the Co-Respondent

When we think of co-respondents in divorce cases, we think of "the other woman," or "the paramour." Technically, the term means a person charged by name in the legal pleadings in the case, the second defendant, the other person who has the right to and should "respond" to the complaint you file. A person, male or female, who has an affair with someone who is married, may find the affair a costly and embarrassing business. Now I'll leave the moralizing on the pains of the adulterous relationship to someone better qualified. From a strictly legal standpoint, the paramour may have his hands full.

Separate and apart from involvement in divorce proceedings, the paramour may be sued for "alienation of affections." Briefly, this cause of action arises when someone is guilty of alienating your spouse, luring him from home and hearth. Married people are entitled to the *consortium* of their spouses; consortium means a spouse's giving of sex, services, and society to the other. When a wife (or husband) is deprived of the mate's *consortium*, she can sue the person who caused it all and, on proving her case, win a judgment of money to compensate her for her loss. Unfortunately, suits for alienation of affections often become tools of blackmail, and consequently, many states have abolished or severely limited the right to bring such a case.

If the adulterous relationship causes a spouse to file for divorce, the paramour may be named as a "co-respondent" in the divorce case. The person suing for divorce will not recover a judgment for money from the co-respondent. Once the co-respondent is named in the suit and served with a summons, she is before the court and may be subject to an injunction. In an effort to save the marriage and bring about genuine reconciliation, judges sometimes will order the paramour and the defendant-spouse to stop seeing each other while the divorce case is pending. The issuance of such an injunction is out of the ordinary, but it can be sought in many states. And people who violate injunctions are in contempt of court and may be sentenced to a stay in jail. Naming the co-respondent—in other words, making her a defendant along with your husband in your divorce case— may give your lawyer broader rights in the "discovery" phase of the case—she will be a party with the duty to come forward with information sought by your lawyer.*

However, unless the "other woman" is utterly without shame, naming her as a co-respondent will undoubtedly be awkward for her. And while it is, at first glance, a tempting prospect to hold her up to ridicule, think twice. First, you'd better be sure you have the right woman before you file a complaint in court compromising her reputation. Second, even if it's definitely the right woman, naming her may accomplish not only her humiliation but your humiliation and that of your children. Third, opportunity for reconciliation may be foreclosed when you force your husband to rise to the woman's defense. If reconciliation is out of the question anyway, the divorce proceeding and its aftermath may produce new lows in animosity. Fourth, naming a co-respondent contains more than the suggestion of vendetta, and if naming her is for the purpose of upping the alimony ante, substitute "blackmail" for "vendetta."

A few state legislatures, recognizing all of these problems, particularly blackmail, prohibit the naming of co-respondents. Other states, apparently on the theory that a person referred to as an adulterer should have both the opportunity and the duty to defend the charge, *require* that the paramour be named as a co-respondent. Most states leave the decision to

---

* The whole subject of "discovery" procedures is discussed in chapter twenty-five.

you and your lawyer and this is yet another occasion when you should rely on professional advice.

If you know your husband is fooling around, but you can't identify the woman beyond "the slinky blonde" or "that woman he met in the bar at the Casa Rendevous," you may, in most states, file for divorce, referring to the lover as "Jane Doe" or "a person or persons unknown." Remember, though, that adultery is very difficult to prove and if the name escapes you, the date and the circumstances must, nevertheless, be at your fingertips.

The Aftermath

Whether it's our Puritan heritage or the gravity of infidelity itself that make adultery the most odious ground for divorce, I cannot say. The fact remains that a man charged with beating his wife often is considered a cut above the man who cheats and gets caught. And if adultery is objectionable in a man found guilty, it is held to be odious in a woman. She may lose custody of her children.* She may be denied of support far more readily than a woman found guilty of any other ground for divorce.**

And there's the scandal. What happens when one charges a spouse with adultery in a court pleading—a public record? Can the couple reconcile? Can they forgive and forget when everyone else in town remembers?

Adultery is the most vindictive, the most difficult to prove, the most humiliating, and probably the most bitter way to end a marriage. Generally, therefore, if you are suing for divorce because of his adultery, try to avoid all the heartache and bitterness by charging him with mental cruelty.

---

* See the chapter on child custody.

** See the chapter on alimony.

7

Conviction of Crime

W<small>HEN</small> a person is convicted of a crime and sentenced to the penitentiary, he trades his name for a number, his plaid sport jacket for prison drab, his evenings out on the town for an afternoon in the exercise yard. In addition to losing his freedom, he may also lose his marriage.

Conviction of a serious crime is, in many states, grounds for divorce. The innocent spouse left at home may sue for divorce because of the partner's conviction. Your husband must have been *convicted*, that is, arrested, tried, and found guilty by a court of law. If he has committed a crime and gotten away with it, then you cannot sue on this ground.

Texas, in 1850, was no place for a woman alone with a baby. Mrs. W remarried hoping for the comfort and protection a husband might offer her and her child. As it turned out, she would have fared better on her own. Mr. W went on a rampage, committing crimes ranging from larceny to murder. In the divorce court, Mrs. W told all, but her husband had never been caught and never convicted. She was denied a divorce on the grounds of conviction of a crime, but the Texas Supreme Court did believe that she suffered mental cruelty and granted her a divorce when she testified that her protector had committed the "cold-blooded and brutal murder of her only son."

Not only must your spouse have been convicted, he must have been convicted *after* you were married. Virginia is one of the few states that allows a divorce on the grounds that your spouse was convicted prior to your marriage and that you married him without knowing of his sordid, criminal past. But in most states, if you married him on the day of his release from Alcatraz, and believed him when he told you he had been doing missionary work in the Congo, he's your husband and you're his wife and there's no grounds for divorce.

If your better half is a campus demonstrator, he may have been "busted" for disorderly conduct. You may have a husband who has been invited by the city to spend a night or two in the "drunk tank." Perhaps he drove without a license or didn't curb your French poodle or found himself in the middle of a scuffle in the tavern down the street. Will an arrest and conviction for any of these brushes with the law give you grounds for divorce? No. Your spouse must have been convicted of a *serious* crime. In order to be certain that the crime was serious enough to warrant divorce, many divorce statutes require that the sentence be of a certain length (usually several years) and that he serve a good portion of it before the divorce is granted. For example, in Hawaii, the sentence must be for life or at least seven years and in Alabama, he must actually have been in jail for at least two years before he can be divorced.

Many divorce laws require that the spouse be convicted of a felony, rather than a misdemeanor. A felony is a crime involving substantial property or threat to another person and is punishable by sentence to a penitentiary rather than a police lockup. Connecticut says the spouse must have been convicted of an "infamous crime involving a violation of a conjugal duty." Assault and attempted rape qualified for Mrs. S's Connecticut divorce. The Georgia statute calls for conviction "for an offense involving moral turpitude." Conviction for the violation of the federal narcotics law involved "moral turpitude." Manslaughter was serious enough for the Indiana divorce court, but a soldier's desertion in wartime and his court martial did not qualify as conviction of an infamous crime. A woman won a divorce when she showed that her husband had been convicted of the rape of a little girl, particularly since the victim was her own daughter.

Let's assume that Joe Hardluck is arrested, tried, convicted, and sentenced. Off he goes to the penitentiary. After a few years, his wife obtains a divorce decree. Then one day a bright young lawyer appears, appeals Joe's conviction, and Joe wins. He is free to walk in the sun once more. His liberty is restored, but not his wife.

And what of Fred Framed? We find him reading his divorce decree while playing soulful harmonica on death row. Just in the nick of time the governor grants a pardon. Fred is absolved of all the consequences of his conviction. His name, his sport jacket, and his nights on the town are his again, but not his wife. Once one is divorced on grounds of criminal conviction, no reversal, pardon, or amnesty will restore the marriage.

8

Gross Neglect of Duty

FOR centuries, at least, each member of the
family had his defined role to play. Even today, when so
many married women are holding down jobs and taking
home salaries, the family members are still likely to see
themselves as fulfilling their traditional duties. The children
go to school, the daddy goes to work, and the mommy takes
care of the household. This division of labor may be insulting
and/or anachronistic, but if daddy or mommy neglects to
perform his or her "duty," he or she may be guilty of grounds
for divorce.

This ground for divorce is called willful or gross neglect
of duty, which seems to be asexual. But in almost all of the
states where this is a ground for divorce, "duty" is defined as
the husband's duty of supporting his wife and "neglect" is
the gross, wanton, or cruel refusal of a man to do so (Maine),
or his "neglect to support his wife according to his means,
station in life, and ability" (New Mexico), or his "persistent

refusal or neglect to provide suitable maintenance for his wife" (Vermont), and so forth. So "duty" is almost always defined as the providing of financial support, and the laws see this "duty" as belonging to the husband.

The duty of support is the husband's duty to provide food, shelter, and clothing, according to his ability. No judge is going to require a husband to provide caviar, a penthouse, and furs—just food, shelter, and clothing. And since you promised to marry for "richer or poorer," it is not grounds for divorce that your husband's dreams haven't come true, that he lost his job, that he is unwell, physically or mentally, and unable to provide for you. He must work at whatever he can to provide for the common necessities, and his failure to provide must be the result of his "idleness, profligacy, or dissipation." It's not that he *can't* work; it's that he *won't*. It wasn't that Mr. S didn't try to provide for Mrs. S. He just couldn't make it. The judge denied her a divorce when he found that Mr. S had always done the best he could and that "bitter misfortune was his sole offending." And, after thirty years of marriage, the chicken farmer's wife failed to prove that her husband was guilty of nonsupport when she "tired of eating chicken and did not care for eggs" and the only fresh vegetables were those grown in the family garden.

Compare those cases to the case of Harry and Barbara and their five children. Harry had a job as an "order picker" at a chain store warehouse. His work was climbing up ladders, carrying down crates of merchandise, loading them on a cart, and climbing the ladder all over again. For ten years, eight hours a day (plus overtime), and five days a week, Harry picked orders, but he was divorced for gross neglect of duty. Every payday, Harry started home with his check, and every payday he stopped off at the local bookie and the local tavern. His salary never made it home. There was no heat, no electricity, no water, no rent money, little food, and ragged, second-hand clothing for his family.

While gross neglect of duty is usually a ground for divorce

for wives suing husbands, there are a few examples where the husband won a divorce against his wife because she neglected to do her duty. An Oklahoma woman was divorced by her husband when she insisted that he pay her a salary to prepare his meals and clean the house, and a New England woman, in 1907, was divorced because she refused to cook meals and, "read frivolous literature to the neglect of her household duties." A Pennsylvania wife's only omission from the performance of her womanly duties was that she wouldn't cook breakfast. Her husband complained that he had to eat cold cereals and sweet rolls. This did not constitute gross neglect of duty.

When Mrs. D sued her husband for divorce on the grounds of mental cruelty because he neither bathed nor changed his underwear for months at a time and spat into a foul, open can next to the bed, she did not get a divorce, but she did get a judicial lecture on her spitefulness in failing to perform her woman's work of cleaning the spit can.

Gross neglect of duty, then, is usually defined to mean a husband's failure to provide and a wife's failure to cook and clean. In Utah, it is grounds for divorce when one spouse fails to provide the other spouse with "the common necessaries of life," and Utah has a specific statute, which states that, without exception, husbands can obtain divorces for the same grounds that wives can use to obtain divorces. Clearly, the "common necessaries of life" are food and shelter, but are they polished furniture, ironed shirts, and scrubbed floors? In North Dakota, a woman who is able to provide support and whose husband cannot work because of illness may be sued for willful neglect if she doesn't use her salary to provide him with the "common necessaries" of life. So far, there's not been a case where a man has won a divorce from his wife because she didn't bring home her paycheck. Until the woman's revolution succeeds, it is not likely that there will be.

9

Habitual Drunkenness
and Drug Addiction

Habitual drunkenness is, according to the divorce law, the "fixed, irresistible custom of frequent indulgence in intoxicating liquor with consequent drunkenness as to evidence a confirmed habit and inability to control the appetite for intoxicants." Or, in other words, he drinks with or without company; he drinks with or without ice cubes; he drinks from a wine glass, water tumbler, or bottle—and he always drinks.

In states where habitual drunkenness is grounds for divorce, you needn't prove that your spouse is constantly, continuously, and unremittingly loaded. You do have to prove that he has a fixed habit of drinking and becoming drunk and that he indulges that habit repeatedly. One woman sued her husband on this ground, but only proved that he was drunk on six occasions during their eight-year marriage. When the judge denied the divorce, her husband was so happy that he went right out and celebrated the seventh occasion.

42

Some states say that the habit must have continued for a definite length of time, at least .one year, or in some states at least two years. Other states call this ground "intemperance," "gross intoxication," or "such confirmed habit so as to make the spouse unable to contribute to the support of the family." It all means that he's a candidate for membership in A.A.

Everyone loves a reformed sinner—and the law is no different. In order to succeed in your divorce suit on the grounds of habitual drunkenness, you must prove that his problem continued right up to the time you filed for divorce. If he was a lush for years, but took the cure when you told him you were considering a divorce, he's yours to keep.

Furthermore, if he was a drunk when you married him, you took him "as is." The habit must have commenced *after* you were married. A man who drinks before he's married, but becomes an earnest drunk after, may be divorced. But when Mrs. W married the drunkard with whom she had lived for three years, she took him as she found him—for good. When a woman married an alcoholic, he sued *her* for divorce, complaining that she refused to let him drink liquor. He was as sober as the judge who denied his right to a divorce.

Drug Addiction

If the use of narcotic drugs was a problem to the American family before the evolution of the "now" culture, no one talked about it. At the turn of the century, a woman could divorce a husband who became inebriated guzzling hooch behind the barn, but there was hardly a divorce law anywhere to help her unload a husband who was addicted to heroin. Things have changed—and the divorce laws have changed, too.

Today, in many states, drug addiction is grounds for divorce. Like drunkenness, the use of drugs must be a confirmed habit. The habit must often have been acquired after the marriage, and, in many states, it must have continued for at least a year or two.

Even the most erudite connoisseur will agree that a drunk is a drunk whether the label is muscatel or brandy. But volumes can be written (and are being written) on just what "drugs" are narcotic drugs, addictive drugs, and habit-forming drugs. Whether marijuana, hash, or cocaine qualify as "dangerous drugs" is a matter lawyers leave to the Food and Drug Administration, the FBI, the college kids, and the talk show hosts. The divorce law says a drug is addictive if it addicts! Whatever he's using, if the drug, weed, or pill becomes a controlling or dominant element in his life, it's addictive and he's an addict.

A New Jersey man left no doubt that he was addicted to heroin when he explained that although he had no desire for sexual relations with his wife, it wasn't that he "loved her less": he simply "loved heroin more."

10

Impotency

Sexual intercourse is a marital right. You are entitled to it—he is entitled to it. When sex is absent from the marriage because of inability, the able, healthy, and frustrated spouse may sue for divorce on the grounds of impotency.

Impotency is a person's inability to have sexual intercourse, the inability to copulate, the inability to insert the penis into the vagina. The legal cases on impotency, with customary simplicity and directness, define it as "incapacity of one of the parties to a marriage for sexual connection," "lacking in physical power to consummate the marriage proceeding from imperfection or malformation," and "inability to gratify sexual desire by the union of the sexual organs of two biological entities."

Impotency is *not* sterility or barrenness, which are inability to procreate, to conceive, to become pregnant. Impotency is *not* the failure to have an orgasm. Impotency is *not* frigidity.

45

You don't have to become pregnant, be able to become pregnant, want sex, or even like sex. Impotency is the *inability* of the husband or wife to engage in sexual intercourse.

Notice that it is the inability of husband *or* wife. Neither sex has a monopoly on impotency. Impotency, when we think about it, talk about it, or tell dirty jokes about it, has become a classy way of describing the inability of a man to have an erection, but there have been plenty of divorces on the grounds of a woman's impotency. One man learned, after his wedding, that his wife was too small, that the introitus, opening to the vagina, was infantile and would not allow him to do more than insert the tip of his penis. The judge agreed with him that this was not enough, that it was not *copula vera* (in Latin, the whole question sounds more dignified), or true sexual intercourse. The wife was impotent and the husband won his divorce.

Divorce law only is concerned with whether the person is impotent, not whether the cause of the impotency is physiological or psychological. Mrs. J was divorced as impotent, not because there was anything physically wrong with her, but because she had a "phobic fear" of sexual intercourse, which caused her to resist, for six years, her husband's efforts to consummate their marriage. When young Mr. K was unable to have intercourse with his wife on their honeymoon, he became so discouraged that he never tried again, and his wife divorced him as impotent.

If your grandchild is reading this chapter aloud to you and you've decided that what you really want for your golden wedding anniversary is a divorce, impotency is not the grounds for you, even if your husband is now truly impotent. To divorce on the ground of impotency, you must usually show that your spouse was impotent *at the time of the marriage and continued to be up to the time of the divorce.* When the preacher told an Oregon bride that her marriage was to be "in sickness or in health," she thought he was giving her a choice. After a few years of marriage, her husband suffered a paralysis that left him impotent and she sued for divorce. Her husband was not impotent at the time of the wedding, so no divorce.

At the turn of the century, in a quiet Pennsylvania town, Mr. and Mrs. Do-It-Yourself lived happily together. Mr. D-I-Y puttered about the house and yard, studied carpentry, gardening, masonry, all the things that meant working with his hands. A true renaissance man, Mr. D-I-Y read up on all subjects—history, science, and the arts. It was no surprise to Mrs. D-I-Y when her devoted husband borrowed several books from the library on the subject of surgery. In fact, she hardly took notice when he took the antiseptic from the medicine chest. The shock came when she found Mr. D-I-Y out in the woodshed shortly after the performance of a perfectly competent and well-executed mutilation and cast-ration—and just think of it, he did it himself! Did Mrs. D-I-Y get a divorce on the grounds of impotency? No. Her husband was capable at the time she married him and that's all the law requires.

A sweet couple met at a retirement village and decided to share their last years, their memories, and their Social Security checks. He was 73, she was 72. After a disappointing three-month marriage, she sued for divorce on the grounds of his impotency and won. The law says a divorce can be granted if a spouse is impotent at the time of the marriage— the judge read the law and followed it.

The judges agree with Oscar Wilde when he said that Niagara Falls is every bride's second greatest disappointment. They know that couples occasionally need a period of adjustment and will rarely grant a divorce to the girl who files her suit before she's written the thank-you notes for her bridal shower. The law, centuries ago, was that no one could sue for divorce on the grounds of impotency until he had been married for three full years, or what the ancient courts called "triennial co-habitation." That's giving it the old college try. Now, we're more sophisticated, and impatient, so divorces have been granted when the marriage was as short as three days.

Ordinarily, though, far more effort is required. One newlywed, on the brink of nervous collapse and suffering from indigestion, testified that for four months her husband was affectionate and teasing. Every night he coaxed her until they were to the point of intercourse, but then—nothing. The judge believed this to be youthful reluctance and sent the couple back to try again.

Let's imagine that you have sued your husband for divorce on the grounds of habitual drunkenness. He denies it. You parade your witnesses—his boss, the neighbors, all the folks who tripped over him in the gutter. If he is guilty of physical cruelty, someone will have seen your black eye. Unless you're an X-rated movie star or really freaky, no one is going to witness your efforts to make love to an impotent husband. How do you prove it?

Mr. G had been divorced by his first wife on the grounds of mental cruelty. He married again and the second Mrs. G soon learned that what her predecessor had suffered from was Mr. G's practice of masturbation. In fact, Mr. G was so addicted to the manly art of self-abuse that his wives were untouched; he was thoroughly impotent where women were concerned. To prove that her husband was impotent, the second Mrs. G asked the first wife to testify. That was a good idea except that in a lawsuit, a former wife can't testify against her previous husband. This is the marital "privilege." Like the lawyer-client privilege and priest-penitent privilege, it is designed to encourage free expression and to preserve confidentiality. The second Mrs. G did, however, manage to obtain a divorce based on her own testimony. The judge believed her. Honest and credible testimony that stands up under questioning by your husband's lawyer is one means of proof, so don't underestimate its importance. One woman sued her husband charging impotency, but did not succeed, when, on cross-examination she admitted that her husband was clumsy but capable.

Because of the physician-patient privilege, it may be difficult to obtain the testimony of the M.D. or psychiatrist who has been treating your spouse, but there may be records or correspondence that can be used at the trial. Courts also have ordered the wife to appear at the office of a court-appointed gynecologist, or the husband to a court-appointed physician, and the failure to keep such an appointment may, in itself, be enough reason for the judge to grant the divorce.

Where impotence is caused by a psychological problem rather than a physical one, proof is all the more difficult. Perhaps you have been treated by your doctor because of the effect on you of your *husband's* impotence. Your physician can testify (if you call your own doctor to the witness stand, you "waive," or give up, the privilege).

As a general rule, in all kinds of lawsuits, not only divorce, you should not decide that although you have been wronged, you cannot sue because you can't prove it. How, or whether, your case may be proved is a professional decision that only a lawyer should make. Tell him the facts, all of them, and let him advise you as to whether or not he can prove your case.

11

Insanity

*"Perhaps it's selfish, Marcia, but I don't want to
share you. I want you for my own."*

*"If only we could run away together, just the two
of us, if only I could marry . . ."*

" . . . Darling . . ." he utters, his chest heaving.

*" . . . but, John, my sweet, you know that I am not
free . . . my husband Bill is in a home for the
incurably insane. I cannot marry you."*

AND so you crunched your popcorn against a
background of swelling violins and poignant emotions erupt-
ing on the silver screen, believing then, as you probably do
now, that insanity is *not* a grounds for divorce.

Yet, in many states, insanity is indeed grounds for divorce,
but it is not an easy ground to prove. It is not the way to get

a "quicky" divorce. Before the law will let Marcia divorce Bill on the grounds of insanity, Marcia must prove that he's not simply a bit neurotic. In fact, if he is less than "insane," she may have difficulty divorcing him on any ground.

For example, after thirty-four years of marriage, a woman suddenly became suspicious of her husband's every move. Her jealousy drove her to follow him everywhere, to throw tantrums, and to make wild and public accusations. He was not flattered and sued her for divorce charging mental cruelty. He lost. The judge decided that her unfounded jealousy was the result of emotional illness and wasn't her fault at all. Another man was excused of his adultery when the judge, borrowing from a Perry Mason episode, ruled that the husband's mental condition made him regard sex as an "irresistible impulse."

To obtain a divorce on the grounds of insanity, one must prove that one's spouse is, has been, or should be confined in an institution because of serious mental illness. The state laws differ, but many of them say that the "insane" spouse must have been institutionalized continuously up until the divorce, and often for as long as five years. The laws also require sworn statements of psychiatrists, chief medical officers, or superintendents that the spouse is "incurably insane" or, at least, that the outlook for recovery is "doubtful."

The law always tries to shelter the children, the aged, and the physically and mentally infirm. The statutes, because they want to protect the person who is accused of insanity, require that the judge appoint a qualified person to represent the accused in court and protect his rights. The law calls this appointed person a "Guardian Ad Litem," a guardian for the purpose of the lawsuit. The GAL may be the district attorney or other public legal officer, or a private attorney chosen by the judge for this particular case. The GAL will defend against the granting of the divorce as if the accused were contesting. He will cross-examine witnesses who claim the defendant's condition is incurable. He may try to prove that the insanity was the fault of the divorcing spouse—that will prevent a divorce for insanity in a few states. He will, if possible, locate witnesses who can testify in favor of the defendant's sanity or that the future looks bright; and, he will try to protect the property interests of his "ward."

The expenses of the trial, including the fees of the GAL, must usually be paid by the spouse who asks for the divorce. If the divorce is granted on the grounds of insanity, the healthy spouse may be ordered to pay for the future medical, housing, and care expenses of the former spouse. In short, the state does its best to see to it that the mentally ill person is not totally abandoned, but is always provided for, even if no longer married.

12

Mental Cruelty

Of all the grounds for divorce, mental cruelty is probably the one women like most—and judges like least. Some states call it "personal indignities" or "inhuman treatment" or just plain "outrages," but however creative your legislature may have been, it's all mental cruelty and, like Omar's tent, it covers a multitude of sins. Sure, there are husbands who beat up their wives and adultery can be a way of life for plenty of men, but women can find their way to the divorce courts without anything so dramatic or hard to prove. The divorce papers filed in court are a public record and even a woman scorned may not want to tell the world that the guy she married won't sleep with her, or urinates in the kitchen sink, or came home from a business trip with a case of VD. Mental cruelty is a distinguished and legalistic rug under which you can sweep all the rotten tricks that you've confided to your best friend, but just can't tell the PTA.

And that's just why the judges don't like it. The conduct that constitutes mental cruelty doesn't fit into boxes the way neat little numbers fit on balance sheets. While almost everyone knows it when they see it, mental cruelty is tough to define.

Nevertheless, the courts have come up with a definition of mental cruelty. This is what it is and this is what you have to prove: "A course of conduct calculated or obviously of a nature to cause such suffering as to endanger health." By "course of conduct" the law is telling you that you're not going to get a divorce because a year ago last Christmas your husband came home drunk from the office party and muttered something about playing post office in the mail room. That will get you a divorce only if it is part of his regular office routine, a "course of conduct." Even then, the conduct must be "calculated" or "obviously of a nature" to be cruel to you. If what he does is "calculated," he has plotted, à la Charles Boyer in *Gaslight*, to drive you wild.

There's the case of the housewife who scrubbed her kitchen floors in the morning and her husband who spat chewing tobacco on them by evening. When she hung her freshly ironed curtains, he washed his hands and face on them, and when she changed the linens, he—well, you get the picture, and that's "calculated." But he doesn't have to be that scheming.

His "course of conduct" may be so obnoxious that it's *bound* to be cruel to you even if he hasn't planned it that way. The farmer's wife had her share of mental cruelty when she caught her husband in the barn making passionate love to a bevy of beautiful sheep. Now that's "obviously of a nature" to result in mental anguish.

Finally, what he does must "endanger your health." Unless you're the neighborhood stoic or a candidate for sainthood, you're bound to be popping tranquilizers by the time you decide to see a lawyer. Your health is endangered if you're sleepless, nervous, or have a good case of the hives. You qualify if your husband gives you an upset stomach, unless, of course, it's because he's taken you to Acapulco. If you've made up your mind to file for divorce, you probably have all of these symptoms and more.

The beauty of mental cruelty as a ground for divorce is that it can include all the dirty deeds one spouse can dream up to hurt another. The list is endless.

Mental cruelty can come from threats of physical violence. Mr. A only intended to scare his wife, he said, when he fired a shotgun at her. Mrs. W sat shaking as she told the judge that her husband had warned that when she was asleep, he'd take his razor to her.

Name-calling can qualify, particularly if the words come from the men's room wall and he uses them to orchestrate your cookie drive meeting. The silent treatment will rarely satisfy the requirements of mental cruelty unless it goes on for months.

There may be days when you believe that your husband promised a bonus to the person who could polish you off. It's an old-fashioned truth that husbands are supposed to protect their wives. If he stands by and watches while his mother attacks you, it's barely possible that you have a case. If he enjoys it, you're closer. If he encourages it, you're divorced. There was the Oregon widower who got a bang out of his kids' shooting their new mama with an air gun. One man used his wife's sickbed for a game of peek a boo with the topless housekeeper.

Unless your husband has a disposition sweeter than Santa or owns a fleet of Greek ships, he's bound to complain about what you spend. Husbands are entitled to complain about charge accounts and phone bills. No judge (who is probably a married man himself) will grant a divorce based only on that. But the wealthy husband who installed his wife in the charity ward when their first child was due went a bit too far.

If your mother said, "You never know a man until you've lived with him," but wouldn't let you live with him until you were married, you may join the ranks of women driven to divorce court by their husband's disgusting personal habits. There was the man who soiled his underwear but refused to change it, the man who blew his nose on the floor, the man who spat in the potted palms, the man who never bathed, or the man who bathed in the front yard of his Pasadena home. One couple is still married because although her husband masturbated in her presence, the judge said she didn't have to watch.

When a nice Jewish boy married a nice Jewish girl, all went well—until he converted. He called her a "lousy Jew" and put religious medals around her neck when she was asleep. On the Day of Atonement, he played the radio as loudly as possible. Today, she toasts bagels for one. Everyone has a right to choose his own religion; you don't give up your constitutional rights when you get married. Nor can your husband berate you for your choice. Mr. R persuaded his wife to join him on a religious commune. She gave all of her property and money to the religious order, but fortunately managed to save enough to hire a lawyer. The sect was vegetarian and refused medical treatment. When their children got the measles, the cure was fasting. Mrs. R went along with all of this until her husband took private "manipulative treatments" prescribed by the daughter of the high priest, who was also the "manipulator."

No matter how inept, unromantic, or dull he may be, sexual intercourse is a "conjugal right." He's entitled to it and so are you. The law does not set standards. No judge is going to schedule your love life or order your husband to bed with you. Sex once a month or once in six months may not be enough for you, but you won't get a divorce unless the need is more extreme. One woman slept alone for twelve years. Another wife waited only one year. A Tennessee marriage lasted only six weeks before it ended in divorce.

Although she tried to teach her young husband, he insisted that sexual intercourse meant rubbing his wife's thighs until he had an orgasm on her nightdress. One man told the judge he wouldn't sleep with his wife because she wouldn't approve of his using contraceptives, but she won her divorce when she testified that the only contraceptives she'd ever seen were the prophylactics he had hidden in the glove compartment of his car. Another Lothario wouldn't have intercourse with his wife because she cracked pistachio nuts in bed. The poor woman was only trying to wake him up.

Mrs. C loved her husband dearly. Their marriage was bliss even though they rarely slept together. He told her that he didn't love her "that way," that their love was something higher, more perfect than a base physical love. Though his income was small, Mr. C was a generous man. He often bought small tokens of affection for his wife and gifts for the clerk who worked in his shop. And yet Mr. and Mrs. C found their way to the Florida divorce court when she surprised her husband locked in naked embrace with his clerk—an appealing teen-age boy.

Mental cruelty can be a discreet means of divorcing a homosexual. Ask Mrs. H, whose husband loved nothing better than dressing in her finest clothes and going dancing with the boys on the Boardwalk in Atlantic City.

Likewise, if the "real" charge is adultery. If he says you're one in a million and you know it's true, you don't have to charge adultery. A married man who can't part with his black book is asking for trouble, but your children don't have to learn that their father did what their Sunday School teacher said Thou Shalt Not Do. You can fall back on reliable mental cruelty. A week at the Mardi Gras ended a marriage when a man left his wife at home but remembered to pack his secretary. A respected suburban doctor, expert in curing chicken pox and mumps, was divorced when his wife caught him practicing adultery by night.

Even if a woman doesn't know that her husband actually

is committing adultery, she can sustain a charge of mental cruelty if he dates other women or stays out late at night without offering a reasonable explanation. Even an old standard like intimate suppers with "the other woman" will suffice.

13

Physical Cruelty

A few years ago, a Southern gentleman, annoyed with the complaints of his pregnant wife, whipped her with a limb cut from a backyard tree. His wife sued him for divorce, and he argued that a man has "the lawful right to whip his wife." The divorce was granted, and the judge declared that a man "has no more right to assault his wife than any other person." That *is* the law. Husbands have no right to strike their wives. A few centuries earlier, the law was different. Then a husband could beat his wife with any rod, switch, hickory—in fact, any weapon, so long as it was narrow enough to pass through his wedding ring. We've all seen Hogarth engravings of pastoral English villages, a woman racing down a winding road, her husband in hot pursuit with a birch rod in hand. Today, our heroine is racing directly to her lawyer's office to file a suit for divorce.

In order to divorce your husband on the grounds of physical cruelty, you must, in most states, prove that he struck you with such violence as either to endanger your life or health or to put you *in fear* that he would endanger your life or health.

Mr. and Mrs. M had been happily married for sixteen years when an attractive widow rented the house across the street. Mrs. M became increasingly jealous of her husband and the widow, even though Mr. M was not the least bit interested in his new neighbor. Unconvinced of her husband's fidelity, Mrs. M's suspicions caused her to start serious arguments and nothing her husband could say or do would quiet her—until, one day, Mr. M became so irritable that he turned his wife over his knee and spanked her. Off she went to her lawyer, filing for divorce on the grounds of physical cruelty, but the divorce was *not* granted. The judge agreed with the lady that the spanking was wholly reprehensible, but it was not of such violence as to endanger her health or even to cause her to be afraid that her health would be threatened. She did not prove such physical violence as would be grounds for divorce.

When a wife bombarded her husband with a jewel box to the head and an ashtray to the shoulder, the court refused the husband a divorce. Again, the judge held that the attacks were not so serious as to endanger the man or to make his life at home unsafe.

The definition of physical cruelty doesn't change whether a woman or a man is inflicting it, but the judges expect a man to withstand a great deal more punishment before they will accept that his wife's acts endangered, or caused him to fear for, his life or health. Thus divorce was denied to the husband whose wife pounded him with the heels of her shoes.

One woman had no trouble at all convincing the judge that she was entitled to a divorce on the grounds of her husband's physical cruelty toward her. During an argument over his mother, her husband grabbed his straight-edge razor. She sped through the house trying to fend him off.

When she grabbed hold of the swinging kitchen door, he slashed her fingers and cut her hands. When she let go of the door, he cut a five-inch gash on her throat. Weak from loss of blood, she fell into the front porch swing, where he continued to slash her until the neighbors arrived. On the day she was released from the hospital, her husband telephoned and said, "Well, good morning, old scout, how are you?" Divorce granted to old scout.

Many states require not only that the assault be a serious threat to safety, but that unless life is threatened, the assaults be *repeated*. The law is that marriages should not be dissolved just because on one isolated occasion a spouse lost his temper and delivered one not-too-damaging attack. With their silver wedding anniversary past and their children grown, Mr. and Mrs. S were ready to enjoy their leisure time, Mr. S with his stamp collection and Mrs. S with her new hobby, charge accounts. When Mrs. S's fascination with charging things got out of hand, Mr. S delivered a sound thump on the back—the first blow in their marriage. No divorce. The judge said the thump was not extreme and certainly not *repeated*.

Another woman was denied a divorce although her husband had slapped her twice. The judge didn't consider the slaps "repeated" since slap number one occurred in one year and slap number two came several years later after an interim of good conduct.

In order for a spouse to inflict cruelty and not be guilty of grounds for divorce, he must prove that his violence was provoked or that he was justified in striking his spouse. In law, a woman does not "provoke" her husband by nagging, quarreling—or even by dating other men. There is a case in Texas that held that a man was justified in beating his wife the morning after she spent the night in a motel room with her boyfriend, but even adultery is rarely said to justify physical cruelty. Another man argued that his wife couldn't win her divorce because since he beat her before they married, she should have expected him to act the same way after their marriage. He lost. A woman has a right to expect her husband to behave.

Is there any justification, then, for physical cruelty? Yes: self-defense. A wife who strikes her husband provokes him to defend himself and he is justified in striking her to hold her off. But self-defense justifies only the use of such power as to protect oneself from the immediate threat. The judges consider the height, weight, and relative strength of the parties in deciding the question of self-defense. A woman who slaps her husband does not give him *carte blanche* to beat her to a pulp.

For example, one lady slapped and spat at her husband, and he hauled off and punched her with his fist. That punch was "unprovoked and unjustified," and he was guilty of physical cruelty. He was allowed only so much reaction as was necessary to protect himself, and he went too far. When a delicate flower flew into a rage and tried to punch her husband, he grabbed her arm, bruising it, and slapped her face. He was *not* guilty of physical cruelty because the judges were convinced that he did no more than was necessary to defend himself.

Mrs. G brought her battered body to her lawyer and sued her husband for divorce. Her husband whined that it was she who was the culprit and that his hand was severely injured by her. The judge learned that this poor mistreated man had beaten his wife, thrown her to the floor, whipped her with a broom handle, and pressed her body against a hot iron. In the midst of all of this, Mrs. G grabbed an egg-beater and hit Mr. G's hand—and that's what he was complaining about. Divorce granted to Mrs. G. She was certainly justified in protecting herself.

Forms of Physical Cruelty

We've said that physical cruelty is, generally, "an unjustified attack, extreme and repeated, which endangers life or health or causes reasonable fear of danger to life or health." The definition is straightforward; physical cruelty, the act, is not. It takes many forms, depending on the devious nature of the spouse, the degree of his temper, and what weapons (or knickknacks, trinkets, or jimcracks) are at hand. Both sexes have enormous ability to inflict harm.

Whenever an Alabama woman settled down to sleep, her husband threw a bucket of water on her. Some men take literally the advice of marriage counselors who tell them to share everything with their wives. Such men, with careful planning and the ultimate in generosity, have shared with their wives all forms of venereal disease. When Mr. L returned from a business trip, his wife asked, "What did you bring me?" Knowing that he had contracted syphilis, Mr. L had sexual intercourse with his wife. What he brought her was a share of his disease. She divorced him on the grounds of physical cruelty. A New England woman divorced her husband because he insisted on having sexual intercourse with her while he was concealing the fact that he was carrying a disease that caused her to suffer "acute urethritis, vaginitis, and chronic catarrhal endometritis." The judge was not in the least sympathetic with the husband's state when he learned that simple cleanliness would have prevented the disease.

Sexual intercourse itself can constitute physical cruelty when it is excessive, as in the case of a farmer's wife who was awakened almost hourly to satisfy her husband's demands. There are a few cases of physical cruelty inflicted by men compelling sexual intercourse with their wives within a few days of childbirth. A Texan was divorced for having sexual intercourse with his wife night and day. He was pleased to tell the judge of his capacity for sex even though he was sixty; his wife was fourteen and seven months pregnant. Mrs. C convinced the court that intercourse once a night was excessive. She and her husband had been married more than thirty years (she was complaining, not bragging). The judge agreed that she was entitled to a rest. Another woman divorced her husband on the grounds of physical cruelty because of his enormous sexual demands upon her, even though she might have expected it. She married at thirty-eight on her groom's eighteenth birthday. (It was *mental* cruelty, not physical cruelty, that ended a marriage when a wife spent all day in bed making unreasonable sexual demands on her husband.)

Psychiatrists, psychologists, analysts, sociologists, and physicians have been writing, speaking, and professing that any sexual behavior that is not painful is normal. According to Kinsey and other researchers, even lawyers and judges probably engage in all of the variations on sexual intercourse that they persist in calling "abnormal." Yet, in law, fellatio and cunnilingus have been considered abnormal and physically cruel. A woman in Pennsylvania divorced her husband because of his commission of these "unnatural sexual offenses." Yet the Supreme Court of Wisconsin denied Mrs. J a divorce a few years ago when she complained of her husband's "abnormal" sexual demands. Mr. J said that cunnilingus and fellatio are not abnormal. In this case the court avoided the issue, deciding that Mrs. J must have consented and so couldn't complain. Faced with the same problem, the judges in Ohio said that in order to claim these acts as physical cruelty, you must prove that the acts were against your will *and* detrimental to your physical or mental health. A "victimized" woman said that fellatio and cunnilingus were physical cruelty, but the judge refused to grant her a divorce. He said that it was difficult to believe that she was an "unwilling participant" in these acts, which took place, as she testified, once a week for eight full years.

Physical cruelty may be the vicious assault of the little woman on the man of the house, and then it's often amusing. Physical cruelty may be the lusty and unremitting sexual demands of one spouse on the other, and then it's a curiosity. But most often, physical cruelty is the angry and violent attack by a man upon his wife, and this is neither amusing nor appealing to the curiosity, unless you're fascinated by the macabre or morbid. Women make their way to their lawyers with blackened eyes, wired jaws, and all varieties of cuts, bruises, and broken bones. This is the stuff of which physical cruelty is made.

Remember, physical cruelty need not be tolerated. A husband has no right or privilege to beat his wife. Unless for some deep psychological reason you enjoy mistreatment, you *can* protect yourself. Call the police, run to a neighbor, lock yourself in and him out. A lawyer can ask the judge for an injunction, a court order, to protect you.* You can divorce the villain, or separate from him, or send him to jail for the night. Or you can wear your bruises with pride and martyr-dom and continue to fend off his blows right up to your golden wedding anniversary. Or you can kiss and make up and never be harmed again. The choices are available, the solution is up to you.

---

* See Chapter 25, dealing with injunctions.

4

14

Voluntary Separation

COUPLES have been known to drift apart. They often decide, between themselves, to go their separate ways. They live in different cities and eventually lose contact with each other. And then there's the case of the "runaway spouse." Husbands, and increasingly wives, have simply disappeared. Are they kidnapped, dead, amnesia victims, or deserters? Where are they? Why have they gone? Can the partner left behind sell the house, cash in the bonds, claim an inheritance, marry again? Since matrimony is a legal status, the law has sought ways and means of answering these questions.

Declaration of Death After Absence
Enoch Arden, according to the poet, Alfred Lord Tennyson, was a "rough sailor's lad" who married his childhood sweetheart, Annie Lee. After seven happy years, Enoch set sail

for China to seek a fortune for his wife and children, telling Annie to "keep . . . a clear fire for me, for I'll be back, my girl, before you know it." Years passed and Annie waited, even years after she had been told that Enoch's ship was lost. Faced with poverty and alone, she relented and married Philip and "Merrily rang the bells . . . But never merrily beat Annie's heart." Enoch, in fact, had not drowned, but had been shipwrecked on an island. Finally, he was rescued and returned. But when he heard of Annie's marriage, and believing her to be happy, he resolved that his wife was "his wife no more" and that he would never tell her or let her know that he was alive. And he kept his promise until the day before he died.

Enoch Arden tells a lovely story and has been the basis for a Broadway musical and a whole series of movies where Irene Dunne, Betty Grable, Doris Day, and Leslie Caron successively found themselves in Annie's predicament. But it doesn't take much imagination to see that as well as being a romantic poem, *Enoch Arden* also presents a legal problem.

Facing up to the legal issue, many states have enacted laws that provide that if a spouse disappears for a period of years (usually seven), and his whereabouts are unknown, and he has totally failed to communicate with any relative or friend, he may be presumed dead. After a court proceeding, his last will goes into effect, the property he held jointly with his wife goes to her, and she can remarry as if she were a widow, with no fear of being accused of bigamy. Laws protect the absentee who is presumed dead by requiring people who receive his property as heirs to post a bond, an insurance policy, with the court. If he returns, he can receive a refund of his property in cash from the insurance company, but he won't receive a refund of his wife.

Not surprisingly, the statutes providing for presumption of death after long absence are called "Enoch Arden laws."

Voluntary Separation

While husbands and wives do go their separate ways, and often don't see each other for months or years at a time, the Enoch Arden laws apply in only a few of these cases. The wife knows her husband is alive and vice versa. She has an idea where he lives and in an emergency can usually get in touch with him. He may have gone to Catalina, but he is rarely shipwrecked.

In such cases, one or the other spouse can sever the legal ties of the state of wedlock and be free to remarry in a "default divorce proceeding." This procedure is discussed in detail in chapter twenty-five, but, in short, the plaintiff (wife or husband) sues for divorce on any of the grounds existing in the state in which he lives. If the defendant doesn't contest, that is, come into court and object to the grant of divorce, the bonds of matrimony will be severed and the husband and wife divorced.

There are, however, a couple of serious problems with the default divorce procedure. Let's assume that our "sailor" took up his separate residence because both parties wanted it that way. He's not guilty of desertion and abandonment. What if he isn't guilty of physical cruelty or adultery, or any of the other grounds for divorce? To prove you are entitled to a divorce, you would certainly have to lie in court. No matter how you try to excuse it, that's perjury. And what if our hero doesn't want a divorce? For one reason or another (religious, financial, to prevent you from marrying his best friend, or because he still loves you), your husband may contest the divorce. So, even if you are willing to perjure yourself: to make up a fairy tale about how he mistreated you, and tell it, under oath, to the judge, your husband may be right there in court with a lawyer and his witnesses swearing it isn't so.

In such cases, it seems that you might be sentenced for life to a marriage that is no marriage at all. Recognizing that marriage with a wife living one place and a husband living another is not a marriage worth preserving, the lawmakers of a handful of states have come up with a grounds for divorce called "voluntary separation."

Voluntary separation statutes provide that if a husband and wife live apart for a substantial period of time, one or the other may apply to the court for a divorce. It makes no difference whether the couple is separated by agreement or whether or not one of the parties is at fault. It makes no difference either if the person *asking* for the divorce is at fault. He may have beat you before he left, but once he's gone for the required time, *he* can divorce *you* for voluntary separation. So, long before California put the divorce laws into a state of shock with no-fault divorce,* many states already had no-fault divorce where the husband and wife had voluntarily separated.

Because voluntary separation is a no-fault-type procedure, the judge will determine only whether the husband and wife have been actually separated for the statutory time period. He will then divide up the property and consider the question of alimony on the basis of the spouses' circumstances, not their guilt or innocence.

Don't be misled though. Voluntary separation statutes are not for "quicky" divorces. You must live at separate addresses for a long time, ranging from one to seven years, depending on the state law.

You must actually live apart during that whole period of time. There will be no voluntary separation as long as you have the same address, even if in all other respects you have nothing to do with each other. For years, the pharmacist's wife lived in an apartment above the store and he lived in a room behind the store. They never dined or slept together, but the judge refused to recognize the arrangement as a

---

* No-fault divorce is discussed in chapter fifteen.

voluntary separation because they kept up the appearance of being happily married for the customers in the store, he had a key to her apartment, and "he used her bathroom regularly." Another woman wanted to divorce her husband after five years of living apart, but was refused a divorce when she admitted that once a month they got together and had sexual relations for old times' sake. But another couple did get a divorce when they convinced the judge that although they shared a hotel bed once or twice during their separation, they did not have intercourse.

15

No Grounds—No-Fault

On January 1, 1970, California had an earthquake. Windows didn't break, rooftops didn't collapse, and Jeanette MacDonald didn't stand amid tons of debris singing heartwarming lyrics about San Francisco. But, in this earthquake, some institutions were shaken up. The California legislature had enacted a no-fault divorce statute.

No-fault divorce says that marriages may be dissolved without proof that a spouse was guilty of any particular misconduct. Grounds for divorce were abolished. In California, it is enough for the seeker of his freedom from the bonds of matrimony to come into the court and to state that he and his spouse have "irreconcilable differences that have caused the irremediable breakdown of the marriage." It makes no difference if, say, the "irreconcilable differences" arise because the husband who wants the divorce wants his secretary, too. It makes no difference if one or both of the parties is at fault. The judge simply hears evidence and makes inquiries, and if he is satisfied that the husband and wife have reached an impasse, the marriage is dissolved.

No-fault divorce is different from mental cruelty. Mental cruelty must be inflicted by the "guilty" spouse if the "innocent" spouse has the right to a divorce. No-fault is also different from the ground of incompatibility. On the surface, "incompatibility" sounds like irreconcilable differences, or rifts in temperament, but even "incompatibility" has been interpreted by the courts to be the result of *fault*. Blame is attached to a "guilty" spouse; the divorce is granted to the innocent spouse. Some states grant a decree of divorce to *both* spouses when blame can be attached to both. Still, blame, guilt, or fault are involved.

In no-fault divorce there is no finding of guilt. There is no blame. It is absolutely forbidden to plead specific acts of misconduct. For example, one doesn't claim that on such and such an occasion, he socked you. One simply claims that the marriage relationship has broken down. Fault or misconduct has no place in the divorce—or, as it is now called, the dissolution—proceeding. The judge will hear evidence of physical cruelty, adultery, drunkenness, and so forth only when there is a contest over who is the fit parent for an award of child custody.

Since California broke the ground, several other states have adopted no-fault or have added no-fault along with the other classical grounds for divorce, and practically every state legislature has considered whether or not to adopt this form. Iowa, for instance, has a no-fault statute where the only ground for divorce is insupportable breakdown of the marriage relationship. Texas, on the other hand, has added no-fault to such grounds as adultery, desertion, and felony conviction. The person filing for divorce takes his choice as to what he wants to plead.

No-fault divorce has been hailed as the welcome end to the myth that in a marriage, one party is guilty and one is a paragon of virtue. No-fault puts an end to the temptation to *create* grounds and commit perjury in order to convince the judge that the marriage should be dissolved because one party's misbehavior fits the legislature's grounds for divorce. With no-fault, a wife can receive alimony based on need and financial circumstances, and it matters not that she be adjudged the innocent victim. No-fault puts an end to the highway robbery that starts with a threat of suit for adultery and ends with the threat to name the lover in the lawsuit and in the newspapers unless the alimony ante is upped. There are, then, powerful reasons for loving, adoring, and enacting no-fault divorce statutes.

But, there's just one problem: No-fault divorce may bring about the irremediable breakdown of the marriage institution. At any given moment, for a good reason or a frivolous one, a spouse may petition the court for dissolution of the marriage. The young man who tires of the obligations of wife and children can simply dissolve the marriage and reduce his duties to writing a check once a month. He need not see his offspring, he need not wipe their bloody noses, sit up with them through the flu, attend the parent-teacher meetings—or give a damn. It doesn't matter that this is a phase dad will grow out of, that his wife loves him, that his children need him. When the grass is greener, he simply writes a check and moves on.

How can a woman defend her marriage from dissolution in a no-fault proceeding? Doesn't it seem fair that if one party seeks to preserve the marriage, the other should then be obliged to prove that because of her misconduct, he's won the right to leave her?

It's an old story that the Moslem sheik could always trim down the size of his harem by choosing his least-favored wife and declaring "I divorce thee" three times. He's got nothing on no-fault divorce.

16

Defenses to Divorce

DIVORCE, aside from its tears, tantrums, recriminations, frustrations, annoyances, aggravations, and irritations, is a legal proceeding. It is a lawsuit. Instead of seeking to win a judgment in money, a jail sentence, or an injunction, the plaintiff is asking the court to grant her a decree of divorce from the defendant. And, like every other lawsuit, the person sued may defend the case and oppose the plaintiff's request for a divorce decree.

The defendant who wins the divorce case wins the right to stay married, and when a woman has hired a lawyer, filed suit for divorce, and gone to trial against her husband, the husband's winning the right to stay married to her may be a hollow victory indeed. This is probably why, although the amount of alimony may be fought with zeal and tenacity, the question of whether a divorce decree should be granted is often not contested in the courtroom.

But this doesn't mean that husbands sued for divorce will

throw up their hands and surrender. Many will contest the suit because they don't want a divorce. Others will threaten to contest the suit, not to hang onto their marriage, but to hang onto their bank accounts. The threat of a contest is the leverage often used by husbands to make the property settlement agreement a little more agreeable. If your husband has a genuinely valid defense to your suit for divorce, he can defeat your efforts to end your marriage, or, at least, hold onto enough of his paycheck to finance his new status as a bachelor.

As any fan of Perry Mason knows, the first defense is that the person accused is innocent. For example, a wife claims her husband beat her and the husband defends and proves that he never laid a hand on her. And there are all sorts of procedural ways to defend lawsuits, like default for failure to answer, motions to strike for refusal to give discovery, and so forth. This is the dryasdust stuff that law and lawyers are made of, and I'm no more inclined to write about the procedural defenses than you are inclined to read about them.

A court cannot even hear a case, let alone decide in your favor, if it doesn't have jurisdiction. This lack of jurisdiction may be another defense and that subject is taken up in chapter eighteen.

In every special area of the law, there are special defenses. For example, personal injury lawyers worry about the defense of contributory negligence. Certain breach of contract suits are lost because of the Statute of Frauds. A patent may be held invalid because the invention was "obvious," and therefore no invention at all.

Because divorce is a special area of the law, it, too, has its special defenses. They are condonation, collusion, recrimination, and connivance. Other defenses, those of Statute of Limitations and Laches, are not unique to divorce law, but can be very important defenses to divorce suits. You may hear about any of these defenses from your lawyer, your husband, or the judge.

The Statute of Limitations and Laches

People are always forgetting telephone numbers, birthdays, which of their children had mumps, and which of their relatives bought them a silver chafing dish and which an electric carving knife. To paraphrase Marc Antony, the good deeds that people do *are* often buried with them—but the slips, the mistakes, the turpitudes, and the shames live on. No married woman is ever going to forget the day, twelve years ago, when her husband slammed the door on her, or the 1937 salesmen's convention in Chicago when he slept with another woman. Therein lies the reason for the married person's tenet that while it may be good for the soul, a confession is hell to live down. Laches and the Statute of Limitations have been created as defenses in divorce suits to help "guilty" spouses live with the tears, the withering glances, and the martyred grimace, and to overcome the eternal threats of divorce that almost inevitably follow that one step out of line.

Statutes of limitations are the laws that tell a person who believes he has a claim or reason to sue someone, that he can't wait around forever until he files that suit. One can't wait until all the witnesses are dead before he sues the bike rider who "demolished" his Cadillac and he can't wait until that cyclist has inherited a fortune, either.

For almost every cause of action in law, there is a statute of limitations that tells you that if you don't file your lawsuit within a certain period of time, you've lost your right forever. But statutes of limitations never have been popular in the field of divorce. After all, a statute of limitations tells a wronged person to hurry up and sue, while the policy of the divorce law is to tell you to forgive and forget, to reconcile, to hold back, and to try to work out your problems.

Many legislators in many states have come to the conclusion, though, that it is a better policy to put a time limit on the whining threats of a wronged spouse.

Statutes of limitations usually say that a plaintiff's suit is forever barred unless he files it in court within a certain number of years from the time the cause of action arose. The cause of action arises when the damaging blow is struck or when the dirty deed done in secret is revealed. For example, in New York, the statute of limitations is five years. If a Flatbush husband beats his wife in 1970, and she doesn't sue him for divorce during the following five years, he's gotten away with it. But, what about the husband who, in the warmth and sentiment of his silver wedding anniversary, confesses to his wife that he slept with a floozie after a bowling banquet eighteen years ago. If she can prove it, she can sue him for divorce on the grounds of adultery. The statute of limitations starts when she *learns* that she's been "wronged."

In the moral, ethical, straitlaced United States, adultery long has been recognized as the most serious ground for divorce. Yet of those states that have statutes of limitations in divorce cases, those statutes often apply only to adultery. So, for example, in Idaho, Oregon, Virginia, and West Virginia, to name a few, there is no statute limiting the right of a woman to sue her husband for cruelty, but there is a statute of limitations on adultery. Now the fact is that when the policy of the law is to punish and stop an illegal act, the statute of limitations is for a long period of time, and when the policy of the law is to make it difficult to sue, to say that the "crime" isn't very serious, the statute of limitations is short. For instance, the statute of limitations on murder may be 100 years and on picking pockets, 1 year. Thus it is odd that adultery, which is said to be the most heinous offense against marriage, often is the only ground subject to a statute of limitations. But there it is.

Laches, like statutes of limitations, is the name for a rule of law that tells a person who believes he has a right to sue, to go directly to court, that is, not "to sleep on his rights." Statutes of limitations are laws passed by legislators with set time periods in them. Laches, on the other hand, is a common-law principle that measures when the plaintiff has waited too long by applying a rule of reason. A judge may say, "Sure, your husband hit you with his pitching wedge because you giggled while he was putting in the 1948 gold cup match at the club. Yes, there were witnesses and you can prove it; yes, there is no statute of limitations that bars your lawsuit. But, it is unreasonable and inequitable for me to grant a divorce for something that happened more than twenty-five years ago. You have rested on your rights—you sat on your cause of action." And that is how laches is applied.

It was laches that prevented a woman from divorcing her husband on the ground of his impotency. He was married to her for seventeen years without sex, and the judge refused her request for a divorce. When an Iowa woman decided to call it quits, she charged her husband with mental cruelty, recounting an argument over a car purchase, the time he threw her clothes into the front yard, and at least a half-dozen other episodes, but no divorce was granted. The incidents were scattered over forty-three years of marriage and the judge sent them back to try for another forty-three. After fifty years of marriage, Mrs. M, a patient woman, decided that she had had enough. Her husband referred to her relatives as "fat little pigs," called her vile names, treated her with contempt and hatred, and attacked her for being of a different religion from his. The judge decided that fifty years was long enough and granted the wife a divorce, saying not a word about limitations or laches.

Condonation
According to the divorce law, time, tide and sexual inter-

course heal all wounds. Condonation is the defense that bars divorce suits because the wronged party forgave the other and so "condoned" the offense. Condonation, according to the law courts, is "the full and free forgiveness, expressed or implied, of an antecedent matrimonial offense on condition that it shall not be repeated and that the offending party shall treat the other with conjugal kindness."

First, condonation is the defense of forgiveness. For example, Jenny and Oliver meet and marry—theirs is an idyllic love story. Then one Sunday, Oliver slugs Jenny. She weeps and says, "Loving someone means never having to say you're sorry." They have sexual intercourse and so Jenny has forgiven, condoned, Oliver's physical cruelty. If their love story ends and Jenny decides to sue for divorce because of the bloody Sunday, Oliver has the defense of condonation and can prevent Jenny from winning a decree.

Forgiveness need not be expressed, but may be implied from behavior alone. That is, a bruised wife does not have to turn to her husband and say, "I forgive you for beating me, I condone what you did." She need only treat him lovingly or forgivingly and she will have condoned the offense and be barred from winning her divorce case. Mrs. J was totally disgusted and appalled by her husband. The brute had raped a fourteen-year old girl. While Mr. J's passions were cooling in jail, Mrs. J sued him for divorce on the grounds of adultery, his having sexual relations with his young victim. But Mrs. J was not allowed to divorce her husband when he successfully defended the suit on the principle of condonation. It seems that Mrs. J had visited her husband in his cell and, in a moment of weakness, made love to him.

Condonation is automatically implied from just one act of sexual intercourse. If the mind is strong and unforgiving, but the flesh is weak, condonation will be a defense to divorce. Alone at last, on their wedding night, the new Mrs. W confessed to her groom that she was pregnant.

Calculating rapidly on his fingers, Mr. W realized that the baby was not his. The next day he filed suit for divorce because of his bride's fraud, but Mr. W did not win his case. After going through the engagement, the ceremony, the receiving line, and the waltz with his new mother-in-law, Mr. W decided he was entitled to sleep with his bride at least once. After she confessed, they made love, and then he left her. That slip left him a married man. And, in another case, Mrs. R lost her suit for divorce although she was separated from her husband for years. She weakened after hearing her husband had come down with the flu and she rushed to his bedside with orange juice, chicken soup, and a shortie nightgown.

So sexual intercourse equals condonation and according to the common law, there can be no condonation without copulation. No matter how understanding, compassionate, or forgiving, a spouse does not condone her husband's guilt of grounds for divorce unless she "proves her love" and has sexual relations with him. One poor soul listened as her husband told all. He described his many adulterous affairs, but his wife loved him still. When she tried to have sexual intercourse with him, he refused. She sued him for divorce on the grounds of adultery and he defended claiming she had tried to make love to him and so condoned the offense. Trying, though, is not sex and not condonation either. She won her divorce.

Even though she was patient and forgiving, a Massachusetts wife did not and could not condone her husband's impotency. But, in another case, there was condonation of Mrs. D's impotence when her husband had sexual intercourse with her "of the kind and to the extent that her condition permitted."

In order for sex to show forgiveness, or condonation, it must, of course, be voluntary. A Midwestern farmer would howl late into the night, until the children begged for quiet, unless his wife would come to his bed. She did not voluntarily condone his cruelty. When her in-laws threatened to take her children and hide them from her, a young mother was forced to accede to their demands that she sleep with their son. She successfully sued him for divorce, although he claimed condonation (and though her in-laws fought, the wife got custody of her children, too). Needless to say, a husband's forcing his wife to have intercourse with him will not be a condonation; Mrs. C did not condone her husband's physical cruelty when she slept with him only after he brandished a butcher knife at the children.

In order to condone an offense, *you have to know about it.* Most wives don't know that their husbands committed adultery on Tuesday when they sleep with them on Wednesday. One very forgiving Alabama woman not only forgave her husband's affair with Miss M but took his and Miss M's baby into her home. Believing her husband's promises to reform, she treated him lovingly and cared for the baby. After another year, Miss M had a second baby, and again, her husband admitted that the baby was his and again promised to repent and stop running around. The Alabama wife forgave her husband and took in his second child, rearing it as her own. And, you guessed it, Miss M had baby number three. But this time there was no forgiveness, there was only a suit for divorce. The wife charged her husband with committing adultery with Miss M and the husband defended the suit claiming that his wife had forgiven him and so condoned the offense. The court agreed that the wife knew of the adultery and condoned it when she forgave her husband after the birth of the first baby, and she knew of the adultery and condoned it after the birth of the second baby. But she never forgave him after she learned of the adultery that resulted in the birth of the third baby. Divorce granted.

It should be pointed out that condonation is *conditional forgiveness* of an antecedent matrimonial offense. When a wife has sexual intercourse with her husband after he raps her in the mouth, she forgives the rap, but not tomorrow's kick, or next Tuesday's slap. Condonation works only on a past, or antecedent, offense. Furthermore, once our hero reverts and commits another matrimonial offense, all former forgiveness and condonation are revoked. The spouse may then complain about every single wrong before, after, or even during the condoning sexual intercourse. So, in order for condonation to be a defense to a divorce suit, the forgiven spouse must not commit another act that would be grounds for divorce. Forgiving is definitely *not* forgetting.

The defense of condonation is, at long last, undergoing a renovation and modernization. Only recently has the divorce law come to recognize that sex may be a temptation and a natural urge and that it may not always mean that a wife is condoning her husband's misconduct. The Missouri Court of Appeals granted a woman a divorce even though she had sexual relations with her husband. The judges decided that their indulging was not forgiveness on her part, but was an "unintentional adventure resulting from propinquity of person and the opportunity it afforded." And a Superior Court granted a woman's suit for divorce even though her husband had teased and cajoled her into bed. The judge said that he acted "premeditatively and fraudulently" with the express purpose of destroying her chance to divorce him. The statutes in Texas allow condonation to be a defense only where the spouse relying on it can prove that there is reason to believe that the couple can be reconciled, and a few years ago, the Vermont legislature absolutely abolished the defense of condonation.

In Illinois, the old-fashioned defense of condonation is still accepted, but the legislature realized that the possibility that a spouse may use that defense keeps couples from even trying to reconcile. The plaintiff is reluctant to risk kissing and making up when her lawyer has warned her that if she sleeps with the defendant, she'll lose her divorce suit. In order to encourage couples to reconcile while still leaving condonation a defense, the Illinois legislature came up with a novel solution, a statute that expressly authorizes copulation during litigation. If an Illinois lady sues her husband for divorce and, while the case is pending, decides that she might want to try again, her lawyer can get a court order suspending the case and allowing all manner of fooling around between husband and wife. The law says that during the life of the order, say thirty days, condonation won't apply.

These modernizations, though, are the exception. The general rule still is that voluntary sexual intercourse after knowing of your spouse's committing an act that would be grounds for divorce is forgiveness, and the defense called condonation may be pleaded to bar your right to a divorce decree.

Collusion

When he was a little boy, he loved to hear bedtime stories. Now he is a grownup and a respected judge in the divorce court and he doesn't want to hear fairy tales anymore.

Collusion is the defense that bars the right to a divorce decree because the husband and wife got together and trumped up grounds. Sometimes the only thing a couple can agree upon is that they want a divorce and occasionally neither of them is guilty of physical or mental cruelty, adultery, desertion, or any other misconduct that is grounds in their state. They sit down and agree that the wife will sue for divorce and though she is testifying under oath in a court of law, she will tell the judge a pure fabrication of her husband's brutality. Her husband will not contest, the divorce will be granted, and they both will live happily and separately ever after.

Collusion is against the law. Remember, there are *three* parties to every divorce case—the husband, the wife, and the state. If the state says a couple may divorce only because of physical cruelty, that's the law and when you enter into the holy and legal state of matrimony, your only escape clause is physical cruelty. Then there's the little matter of perjury. It's an unpleasant practice and a criminal act as well.

Consider the possibilities. You go to the divorce court to tell your fairy tale. Your husband changes his mind. He's not going to let you tell the world he deserted you when he didn't and he doesn't want a divorce anyway. He raises the defense of collusion and, at best, you're denied a divorce; at worst, you're charged with perjury.

Or let's assume that the little scheme is flawless. On to the witness stand you go, the clerk swears you in, and you start telling just a bit less than the whole truth and nothing but. The judge hears divorce cases from 10:00 A.M. to 4:00 P.M., five days a week, year in and year out. He may sense a bit of inconsistency, a professional poise in your delivery, a story too pat to be true. He may deny your divorce on the grounds of collusion and again, there's the little matter of perjury.

Remember, though, that collusion is creating grounds that don't exist. If your husband really is guilty of grounds for divorce, and you sue him, and he decides or even agrees not to defend the case, that is not collusion. Anyone who is sued has a right to go to court or stay at home, defend or not defend the lawsuit, as he or she chooses. It is only when you *conspire* to play a trick on the state and fabricate grounds that you are guilty of collusion.

Also, on occasion, a court will refuse to enter a divorce decree when the grounds are genuine, but the plaintiff truly wants to stay married, and has been cajoled, pressured, or defrauded into suing for divorce. A Hawaiian woman loved her husband even though she knew he was keeping a wahine on the side. Her husband made an appointment with a lawyer for his wife, paid the lawyer, and convinced his wife that she should divorce him. At the trial, the wife said that she never wanted a divorce at all. The judge then denied the divorce on the defense of collusion because it was clear to him that the suit was being prosecuted solely for the benefit of the guilty husband.

An Oregon husband was more direct. He wanted a divorce so that he could marry his girl friend, and he filed for it. His wife never came to court to defend. The divorce was granted and Don Juan married wife number two. It was only when they left town on their honeymoon that the first wife got the courage to hire a lawyer. She and her lawyer went to court to prove that the only reason she didn't defend the divorce suit was that her husband had threatened her with "great bodily injury or death" and promised to "get rid" of her if she stood in the way of his marrying his steady girl. The judge heard both sides and ruled that the husband's suit for divorce was a fraud on the state. He set aside the divorce, which, by the way, left wife number two the second wife of a bigamist and not a wife at all. The law and its judges don't like to be made the butt of little jokes.

A Florida wife swap led to a double-header collusion. Mr. and Mrs. H and Mr. and Mrs. W decided they would be happier if Mr. H married Mrs. W, and vice versa. They decided on a double divorce. Mrs. H filed first, Mr. H didn't defend, and Mrs. H got her decree. Then she took a long, hard look at the property settlement agreement she had made with her husband, and a long, hard look at Mr. W, and decided that neither amounted to very much. Back to court she went. She told the judge the whole tawdry story and that she and her husband had colluded in creating grounds and that now that she was divorced she had changed her mind. The judge would have none of it. He concluded that she agreed to "play a trick on the court" and that when she realized her husband had got the better deal, she changed her mind. He refused to set aside the divorce. She got the divorce and she was stuck with it.

Since the policy of the state and the dignity of its courts are involved, both the legislature and the judges keep a watchful eye for signs of collusion. Illinois law says that if a divorce suit is not contested, the plaintiff must produce two witnesses who will testify under oath that the grounds are genuine. Michigan courts refuse to grant a divorce unless the plaintiff does "solemnly swear that there is no collusion, understanding, or agreement . . . in relation to the application for divorce." In Hawaii, the judge can investigate a suspicious suit for divorce and in Massachusetts, there is a stiff fine or jail term for the fraudulent procuring of divorce.

If a person charged with adultery comes to court and readily agrees that he certainly is guilty, the judges are likely to be suspicious. It is not unusual for couples to arrange for the husband to be photographed in a compromising position with an attractive woman. When the photographers burst into a hotel room, the husband should not calmly order three 8 × 10's and a half-dozen wallet-size prints. Adultery confessions are viewed with a jaundiced eye, and in some states, Alaska, for example, a divorce will never be granted on the basis of defendant's confession alone. West Virginia courts will not grant divorces for adultery on the voluntary confession of "a prostitute" or the other woman.

I won't tell fairy tales, either. It has become the practice in some states (particularly the "quicky" divorce states) and in some courtrooms (particularly where there is a broadminded judge who is at odds with his state legislature's narrowminded position on divorce) to award divorces even where collusion is pretty obvious. This sort of thing subverts the law rather than honestly changing it. It encourages a disrespect for the law and leads people to think that when it's convenient, they might as well perjure themselves.

As a practical matter, in this day of mental cruelty, incompatibility, and no-fault divorce, collusion isn't even a *necessary* evil. When two people *want* a divorce, real, honest-to-goodness grounds exist. The grounds need only be pleaded, not created.

Recrimination

If you lived in Elizabethan England and someone rear-ended your coach and four, you would apply to the Queen's courts and receive a judgment for money to compensate you for your bent carriage fender. If you wanted special relief, or an "extraordinary writ," you would apply to the Chancellor's Court. The chancellor, the keeper of the Crown's conscience, would listen to both sides of a case and fashion the relief to fit the case—for example, an order requiring the return of the family jewels, an injunction, or a divorce decree. The chancellor would not simply dole out a money judgment; he would do what was *equitable* under the circumstances of the case.

The situation today is identical. If you sue for divorce, your lawyer will file your suit in the divorce division of the Chancery or Equity court. If you win your case, the judge, or chancellor, will fashion a divorce decree that is equitable under the circumstances of your particular case.

There are unique requirements before one can win a suit in an equity court. Perhaps you've already heard the maxims, "He who seeks equity must do equity" and "He who comes into a court of equity must come with clean hands." All of this means, simply, that one who asks for the special relief of an equity court must not be a wrongdoer himself. He must be blameless in the case—he must have clean hands.

That is the history that forms the basis of the divorce defense known as recrimination. If you seek a divorce decree, you must not have been guilty of grounds for divorce yourself. No matter how badly your husband may have treated you, if you sue him for divorce, he may defend that you are not entitled to the equitable relief of a divorce decree because you also have been guilty of misconduct amounting to grounds for divorce. That is unclean hands, or the defense of recrimination.

It must be remembered, of course, that anytime a spouse successfully defends his mate's right to a divorce, what he wins is the right to stay married. It is pretty obvious then why the defendant in a divorce case may conveniently "forget" to defend on the basis of his spouse's misconduct. This is not to say that it doesn't happen. Mrs. S sued her burglar husband because he had been convicted of a felony and imprisoned. He defended because she was living in the woman's reformatory (she drove the getaway car). A New Jersey wife wanted a divorce because of her husband's adultery, but he proved that she, too, had been fooling around, and with his brother. She had not only been indiscreet with her in-law, but she had managed to pick up his "skin disease" and had left her panties in his bed.

When an Arkansas man tried to defend against his wife's claim that he had beaten her, he told the judge that she had infected him with syphilis. The judge didn't believe his story when he learned that the man had contracted both syphilis and gonorrhea when his wife was out of town. Another couple, Mr. and Mrs. K, are still married even though she had been a shrew, accusing him of improper sexual relations with his daughter. He pushed her around, had his children torment her, and falsely accused her of trying to poison them. When her husband slapped her, Mrs. U went to the Alabama Supreme Court for a divorce. But the judges looked at the evidence—she outweighed her husband and generally got the better of him in their fistfights.

Because of the defense of recrimination, many couples are still married to each other. Their marriages may be intact, but I doubt that their homes are. Unable to divorce because of their both having committed adultery, Mr. and Mrs. M decided at least to live apart. Because they were both guilty, the court decided neither was a fit parent entitled to custody of their children. The boys were awarded to their adulterous dad and the girls went with their adulterous mother, and everyone suffered.

While recrimination has a logical basis in the historical

context of the equity courts, it just isn't a realistic approach to marital problems, and certainly does not provide a solution. Keeping a man and woman under the same roof when at least one wants a divorce and both are guilty of grounds for divorce is, at best, an exercise in futility and, at worst, an invitation to open warfare and let the children be damned.

With this in mind, a few states, Vermont and Texas, for example, have absolutely abolished the defense of recrimination. But this isn't a solution, either. It simply means that a guilty husband may force a guilty wife to sue for divorce. If he files for divorce and her only defense is his equal guilt, recrimination, she cannot plead that defense and bar the right to divorce. To preserve her claim to support, child custody, and so forth, she must countersue for divorce. Abolishing the defense of recrimination may mean that a spouse who wishes to wait, work things out, and reconcile may be pushed to the courthouse by an equally guilty mate.

Illinois' solution to the recrimination confusion is a compromise with the Old English law. Illinois still recognizes recrimination as a defense, but the judge is not allowed to deny a divorce unless the defendant actually comes to court and specifically pleads his spouse's guilt. If he doesn't plead recrimination, the divorce judge cannot bar the plaintiff's right to a divorce.

For example, a wife sued her husband for divorce charging adultery. He had, she claimed, been the father of her sister's three illegitimate children. The husband did not contest his wife's right to a divorce, being delighted at the prospect of having their marriage dissolved, but he argued that she, too, was guilty of adultery and so she should be denied alimony. When the judge heard this, he denied not only alimony, but the right to a divorce, leaving them husband and wife. In the appeals court, the judges said that as long as the husband didn't specifically plead recrimination as a defense to bar her right to a divorce, her guilt should be considered only in deciding whether she might get alimony, but should not bar her right to a divorce.

Along similar lines, some state legislatures, like Oregon and Colorado, have abolished recrimination, replacing it with the doctrine of "comparative rectitude." Under this doctrine, the judge will listen to both stories and award a decree of divorce to the spouse who is "less guilty." The judge then compares the rightness of the plaintiff with the wrongness of the defendant. Sometimes the comparison results in the judge simply awarding the decree of divorce to *both* parties.

And so the experimentation goes on. But the early, common-law defense of recrimination still prevails. When a woman decides to sue her husband for divorce and is first interviewed by her lawyer, he will ask her what awful things her husband did—and he also will ask if she is guilty of misconduct amounting to grounds for divorce. He is not being nosey, he simply wants to know if the husband will be able to defend the case and if his client will be entering a court of equity with clean hands.

Connivance

A man may have a perfect wife, whom he can't divorce, and a perfect lover, whom he longs to marry. His first plan is to tell his wife of his adultery and ask her for a divorce. Failing that, he treats his wife with disdain, then with cruelty, trying to compel her to a lawyer's office. If she is steadfastly determined to remain his wife, he might try yet another course of action. He will scheme, plan, and arrange for his wife to misbehave. He will ensnare her into an offense. He will "connive" at her guilt of grounds and having succeeded in trapping her, sue her for divorce. Even this course of action may fail, though, for a defendant in a divorce case who has been entrapped by the plaintiff into violating her marriage vows, may defend the suit using the defense of "connivance."

Connivance is the defense that says that a divorce will not be granted to a spouse who has corruptly consented to or actively procured his mate's commission of the grounds on which he bases his divorce case. If a wife is suspicious of her husband's misconduct, but takes no action to prevent it, she may be passive, dull, docile, or uninterested, but she has *not* connived at his misconduct. She must have arranged her husband's date, procured the bait, and caught him in her trap, then she has connived and he may defend. A husband who puts his wife on the streets, exposes her to lewd companions, or, as in the case of *B* v. *B*, makes himself a pimp and his wife a prostitute, cannot then successfully charge her with adultery. He has connived at her adultery and she can then defend his suit.

Mr. M hired a detective to spy on his wife, hoping that he would find her committing adultery. For days the detective followed Mrs. M to the supermarket, the laundromat, a PTA meeting, and a Scout rally, and he waited outside for hours while she played bridge with the girls. Disgusted and impatient, Mr. M offered the detective a bonus if *he* would seduce the woman. The detective earned his bonus, but Mrs. M is still married, having proven that her husband connived to procure the grounds to sue her for divorce. Mr. and Mrs. G spent the evening with a bachelor friend. Mr. G complained that his wife was "undersexed" and told her she should find a lover. Off she and the bachelor went and had an "oversexed" evening. No divorce for Mr. G, who had encouraged and procured the adultery. And there was the Pennsylvania woman who hired a call girl to entice her husband into an embarrassing pose for her photographers. All of this was carefully planned to help the woman do better in the property settlement agreement, but no divorce means no alimony either.

Connivance is most often used as a defense where the grounds are adultery, but this is not always the case. One woman was denied a divorce because she had planned and conspired in the armed robbery that caused her husband to be a convicted felon. A New England woman was an admitted alcoholic. She sincerely tried to go on the wagon, but her husband, who sued her as a habitual drunk, brought bottles of liquor home every evening and took her to one tavern after another.

Arranging for your spouse's drunkenness, criminality, or adultery means simply that you may be married forever to a drunk, a criminal, or an adulterer. One cannot obtain a divorce at his convenience by procuring, ensnaring, and, thus, "conniving" in his mate's misconduct.

These are the classical defenses to divorce: statute of limitations, laches, condonation, collusion, recrimination, and connivance. A successful defense may mean the preservation of an unsuccessful marriage. There is always the possibility, though, that a successful defense means a serious effort at reconciliation.

17

Your Lawyer and
Your Lawyer's Fee

Everybody knows what a dentist does. He
drills teeth, asks you your philosophy of life when your
gums are stuffed with cotton balls, and plays golf every
Wednesday. Everybody knows what a physician does. He
listens to your heartbeat with an ice-cold stethoscope, goes
to Hawaii when you go into labor, and plays golf every
Wednesday. And everybody knows what lawyers do. They
write on long, yellow tablets, they use words you can't
understand, they put criminals on the streets to rape your
daughters, and they play golf every chance they get.

Finding a Lawyer

How do you find a lawyer? Who is a good one? How do you
know that this is a person in whom you can place your
trust and confidence? One thing is sure. You won't find the
lawyer of your dreams in an advertisement on the side of a
bus. Attorneys at law don't advertise. It's unprofessional and

93

unethical. The closest they get is the sending of Christmas cards to clients and friends and pristine, little announcement cards when they move their offices or switch their partnerships.

In the divorce field, the view of the law is that marriage is a state worth preserving and woe to the lawyer who runs a commercial message telling the public to rush in for a divorce. The West Virginia, South Carolina, Ohio, Minnesota, and Illinois divorce laws, among others, provide that a lawyer who advertises, circulates, distributes, or publishes with the idea of procuring divorces or divorce business can go to jail, or be fined, or be disbarred, or all of the above. A Nebraska lawyer was suspended from practicing law because he ran an ad in the local paper offering divorces at a cut rate and a Minnesota attorney was tracked down by the state through the box number he used in a magazine ad.

But since you won't find divorce lawyers the way you find plumbers, by looking for the splashiest ad in the classified phone directory, where do you turn?

The ideal situation would seem to be the one in which you have a lawyer who has handled your affairs for years. He knows you and you know him. Such a lawyer is likely to be your "family" lawyer. That is, he has represented both you and your husband. However, if you want counseling for separate maintenance or divorce, he may not be the person you should turn to now. Even the most friendly divorce, if there is such a thing, requires a lawyer who is *your* advocate. He must represent one spouse, not both. This is not to say that a lawyer may not represent both husband and wife (and many perfectly ethical lawyers will do that so long as their clients know and understand that he will be serving two masters).

Usually in the course of the suit or in the drafting of the property settlement agreement, or in the determining of who sees the children on Christmas, the best situation is the one where your lawyer represents you and his lawyer represents him. That's *advocacy,* and until we reach the time when personal facts can be fed into a computer, and justice rolls forth on the printout, advocacy is the best system we've got for achieving a fair result. Your family lawyer may well find it impossible to represent one of his clients against another and so, in a divorce situation, may decline to represent either of you. And that still leaves you without a lawyer.

Very often your family lawyer will recommend to you another member of the bar. Assuming that the recommending lawyer is someone you know and respect, he will not suggest the name of a colleague who is inept or dishonest. Lawyers often know personally, or by reputation, hundreds or even thousands of their colleagues. If one attorney recommends another, he is often placing himself in a position of endorsing the other, so he won't make the recommendation lightly.

Then there's the lawyer recommended by your friends. Here, it's the judgment of your friends that you have to analyze. Does your friend actually know the lawyer? Has he or she used that lawyer's professional services? If your friend's relationship to the lawyer is only that he is the first cousin of her hairdresser, that's very different from your friend giving you the name of a lawyer he or she has hired, dealt with, and relied upon.

The problem of finding a lawyer may be simplified, or, on the other hand, compounded, if you're from a small town. In a small town, you may know personally or by reputation all of the members of the bar. So much the better. Choose the best and call for an appointment. But if everyone knows the attorneys, the attorney may know everyone, including your husband. And, when advocacy is at stake, it's best not to rely on the attorney your husband drinks with. What more horrifying picture can you conjure up than *your* lawyer and *your* husband sitting in a steam room discussing *you.* In such cases, it may be necessary to go off to the nearest town or city to find your lawyer.

If you live in a city of any size and are without personal sources for legal help, look up the telephone number of the city bar association. A bar association is more than an exclusive dining place and a law library. It provides a number of services, such as recommending new or revised statutes to the legislature, studying new approaches and procedures, keeping lawyers abreast of the latest cases, and, most important to you, receiving and investigating grievances on professional misconduct and maintaining services for referring people to attorneys with experience in particular fields.

With regard to the question of experience in particular fields—do you need a "divorce lawyer" to handle your divorce case?—opinions differ. Experience is valuable in any field, so the man who handles divorce cases every hour of every day has an edge. But the client in the office of a divorce lawyer can sometimes be fed through the machine—she's just another divorce case; we've filed them before, we'll file them again. Take a number, wait your turn, and unless you have plenty of money, you may never see Mr. Big anyway. What a divorcing wife (and every other client in every other case) needs is an attorney who knows his stuff, isn't afraid to learn more, and performs professionally. So if you hire a tax lawyer to handle your divorce case, and he knows what he has to do and does it well, it is of no consequence whether he has a big reputation with the divorce bar. And if you've got the most famous divorce lawyer in the city, but he never returns your phone calls and can hardly remember your name, well, so much for the big time.

The sources for lawyers then are other lawyers, their clients, and the city bar association. All of this boils down to reputation. A lawyer worth anything will value his reputation and won't gamble it, even if there's a fat fee for the risk. Once you have a lawyer's name, it never hurts to ask around and find out what people who know him think.

The Fee and the Costs of Suit

Now that you've found a wonderful lawyer, with the finest reputation and the greatest of skill, you'll have to pay him. You'll pay him because he's using skill and drawing on that reputation and because—you've heard this before—a lawyer's time and advice are his stock in trade. You wouldn't think of walking into a department store, picking a few items off the counter, and walking out without paying. Likewise, when a lawyer advises a client, he is giving out some of his "inventory," and he deserves to have his bill paid—even if you change your mind and decide to stay married. If he brings about a reconciliation (and if he's any good, he's bound to explore the possibility of bringing peace to the family), he is performing a service, spending his time, and must be paid. Accept, then, that the attorney must be paid, then settle the questions of how much and how often he will get his money.

Don't be shy. At the very first meeting with a lawyer, a client should learn what he will charge. The lawyer should be able to quote a fee and he should prepare a letter agreement at that time stating that he will represent you and that you will pay him a certain amount.

Lawyers bill their clients on four different bases and sometimes a combination of the four. First, a lawyer may charge a *retainer*. That is, he will take a flat fee in advance and do all of the legal work you give him for the next year, and then he'll send another statement and do all of the legal work for the succeeding year, and so forth. This retainer system is just grand if the client is a corporation that wants a lawyer around to handle whatever problems come up, but unless you marry and divorce whenever the moon is full, this system is not for you.

The second basis is called the *contingent fee.* Here the attorney shares with his client whatever he recovers for her. One day, Miss S, while streetwalking, gets nicked by a half-ton truck. She sues the truck driver, the trucking company, and anyone else around, for a hundred thousand dollars. If she settles the case for $10,000, her lawyer picks up his contingent fee; for example, one-third, or $3,333.33. If, at the trial, the truck driver proves that he had stopped at a light and that Miss S wiggled right into his bumper, and if Miss S gets no money at all, her lawyer still gets his third, and a third of nothing is nothing.

Contingent fees often provide the means whereby a person who can't afford to pay a lawyer can be represented. A contingent fee might sound very appealing to the client without ready cash. But even if the cookie jar is empty, don't try to arrange a contingent fee with a divorce lawyer. In theory, he could get a third of the alimony and child support payments, or a third of the value of the property settlement. In practice, he cannot, because the ethics of the profession and the law in most states forbid a lawyer to take a divorce case on a contingent fee basis. First, a lawyer paid one-third of the alimony will be unlikely to try for a reconciliation. The law thinks that the preservation of marriage is desirable, even if you don't, so no fee arrangement can be approved that tends to encourage the dissolution of marriage. Second, when a court awards alimony, it's awarding an allowance reasonable to support a spouse considering her needs and circumstances. The court is not figuring in the support of a lawyer for life. So, the contingent fee is out —and the lawyer who suggests it is either uninformed or a shade unethical. Run to the nearest exit.

The third fee arrangement is the *hourly rate.* When a lawyer takes on a case that looks easy, it often turns difficult. A one-day trial may go on for weeks, be brought to the Court of Appeals, the Supreme Court, back again, merit a new trial, and so forth. In fact, attorneys have been known to pale at just hearing a client tell them about "a real simple little case where you can pick up a few hundred bucks." Because cases vary in complexity, lawyers charge on an hourly rate basis. The open-and-shut cases taking a few hours are billed small amounts; the tortuous, worrisome cases can result in sizable bills every month.

A lawyer's hourly rate varies with the case, the client, the part of the country, and, principally, the lawyer himself. A man at the height of his career can and should charge more than a beginner or a venerable elderly practitioner. A lawyer with the finest reputation, a super brain, and an elegant reception room may charge more than his colleague down the street. Hourly rates vary, but in divorce cases $25.00 an hour is cheap, $40.00 per is about average.

The fourth fee system is the *flat fee*. The lawyer hears your story, does some mental gymnastics (generally, figuring an hourly rate and estimating the time he'll put in), and quotes a fee for the suit from start to finish. One of the major city bar associations suggests that a flat fee be in the area of $400 for the uncontested divorce to $1,000 for the involved contest, and an additional $300 for every day of trial.

The fee, and that's what we've been talking about, does *not* include the *costs of suit*. Those costs are the separate out-of-pocket expenses that the client must pay. Again, a lawyer's advancing the costs or paying them himself is a tinge improper. He is encouraging the pressing of the suit. If you want it, you pay for it.

The first cost is the fee for filing the case, which is paid to the clerk of the court ($20.00 to $40.00). There is also a fee to the sheriff, marshal, or bailiff for serving the summons ($6.00 to $25.00). Court reporters must be paid for taking down legal arguments or testimony and typing up their notes (the transcript). A full day of testimony may result in a court reporter's fee of $100 (most divorce trials run only an hour or two, so don't panic). If you win a decree, you'll want an official (certified) copy to gather dust in a safe deposit box, shoe box, or bottom bureau drawer ($10.00). If you *don't* win a decree and decide to appeal, there's the printing of the briefs on appeal and filing fees in the courts of appeal and so forth—all of which can amount to staggering sums.

Who Pays?

If, as you've been learning about lawyer's fees and costs of suit, you've been emptying old purses looking for forgotten money and finding linty Lifesavers instead, or if you've slipped into your son's room to size up his coin collection, or if you've added up all of your assets for a grand total that's not worth discussing, take heart.

The law recognizes that, traditionally, daddy earns the money and mommy takes care of the household. It recognizes, too, that in that situation, a husband suing his wife for divorce, or defending her suit, can pay a lawyer a fee and leave his wife with no lawyer at all. A man with a substantial salary may hire a firm of smart, smooth, well-connected pin-stripes and his wife may have no more than the advice of the law school freshman who used to mow their lawn.

This just isn't fair. So, if the wife is without the means to hire a lawyer for her divorce suit, she may hire a lawyer by paying him a small retainer, or, perhaps, just enough to file the suit. After the husband is served with the summons, and quicker than you can say "payable in three installments at 30, 60, and 90 days," the wife's lawyer may move the court for an award of fees while the case is pending. The judge will consider the husband's salary and obligations and order the husband to make payments to the wife or to the wife's lawyer for legal services during the time the suit is pending in court.

If the wife has cash on the side, a steady job, or a few parcels of downtown real estate, she will have to pay for her lawyer out of her own pocket. And if the husband stays home and the wife works, most states will require that the wife pay the husband's attorney's fees. So the purpose of the award of fees is *not* to penalize the poor male, *nor* to line the lawyer's pockets. The award of fees is to put husband and wife on an equal footing so both may prosecute and defend without having the balance tipped in favor of the spouse who works outside the home.

Expectations

Unlike the laundry down the street, your lawyer may not always provide same-day service. A lawyer may see a client for one hour. But when the client leaves the office, he usually leaves behind him hours and weeks of paperwork. And even though you're terribly important, you're not your lawyer's only client.

This doesn't mean that your lawyer is excused from working diligently and efficiently on your case. Nor does it excuse the lawyer who doesn't return your phone call.* And when you have an appointment to see your lawyer, he should treat you as if you were his only client. It is simply that the law courts grind out justice at a slow but steady pace. The lightning-quickest lawyer still has to operate within the judicial system, and that takes time. Then, too, the waiting game may help you. While the case is hung up in court, your husband may get hung up on another woman and give up his contest. Or, you and he may decide that marriage is better than all this divorce nonsense and reconcile. Anything may happen.

Be honest with your lawyer. Tell all. It's an unpleasant surprise for a lawyer pressing a suit for a demure housewife in gingham to learn at the trial that she supplements her

---

*One way to get excellent treatment is to keep your calls to a minimum. Think before you grab the phone to call your lawyer; you may not need to bother him. If your conversations have been significant, your calls should be promptly returned.

Christmas Club savings by dabbling in prostitution. The lawyer who knows the bitter truth can defend, omit, or finesse it.

Don't ask your lawyer to create your case or find the evidence to support it. Attorneys are not private eyes. They are members of a learned profession and eavesdropping, wiretapping, tape recording, and keyhole peeping are not their game. Most wiretap evidence isn't acceptable as courtroom testimony anyway, and the ethics of the profession require that a lawyer be an advocate, *not* a witness. Even if he should find out all the juicy details about your husband, he'll probably never be able to take the witness stand in your case. Your lawyer, if he's any good, won't work out a collusive divorce, won't teach you to lie on the witness stand, and will not provide you with "witnesses" from among his secretarial staff. If you've hired a lawyer who prides himself on making your case easier by bending the law, you've not only hired a shyster, but you've probably got yourself a man who doesn't know how to win a case legitimately.

So you've found a lawyer, you've paid him—now let him do his job. Patients don't tell their dentists which teeth to crown and they don't design the incision for their appendectomies. Put a client in a law office and you've got an instant expert on the law, the judiciary, the how to, when, and why. Read this book, read the next divorce book, study the law in fifty states, in Washington and Puerto Rico, engrave the grounds for divorce on the head of a pin if you wish—but when you've finished, you still won't be a lawyer. By the way, even a regular licensed lawyer wouldn't be pigheaded enough to represent himself.

Trust your judgment in selecting a lawyer, then trust the lawyer.

18

Where to Sue for Divorce

IF you're an efficient, budget-conscious, quality-demanding American woman, you're likely to think about shopping around before you choose a court in which to file your suit for divorce.

After all, why not choose a state with a kindly judge who loves nothing better than granting alimony? Sue in a town where the lawyers are billing their clients at cut rate? Why bother with the states that may deny a divorce because of an Old English defense? And, if grounds are a problem, why not file in California for a no-fault divorce? Well, why not? Simply because although shopping around may be the time-honored way to buy hamburger, when you're filing a lawsuit, there's the little matter of the U.S. Constitution and the legal principle of jurisdiction to take into account.

You exercise jurisdiction when you forbid your children's playmates from finger painting on your silk bedspread. Your husband exercises jurisdiction when he bans you from using his razor. And the pastor exercised his jurisdiction, when, by the power and authority vested in him, he declared you man and wife. Jurisdiction is, literally translated, "the right to speak."

Divorce lawyers have three kinds of jurisdiction to worry about: jurisdiction over the subject matter of a divorce case, personal jurisdiction over the husband and wife in the case, and jurisdiction over the status of the marriage. When you put them all together, you have the court where you file your suit, and there's not much shopping around.

Jurisdiction Over the Subject Matter

The court that has the authority to hear evidence and decide a particular case has jurisdiction over the subject matter of the case. You don't defend a parking ticket case in the Supreme Court, you go to the traffic court. You don't ask a justice of the peace to give you an income tax refund, you go to the federal district court. No matter how base and corrupt your husband may be, you don't sue him for divorce in the criminal court. Your lawyer will file your suit in the "divorce court," the court that has jurisdiction over the subject of divorce.

Depending on the state law, that court may be the county district court, the circuit court, or the court of common pleas. It will be a court of equity: a court of equity has the power to do more than give a judgment for money, and is a court where the judge may fashion the remedy to fit the specific offense. Where the offense is guilt of grounds for divorce, the remedy will be a decree of divorce dividing up the family fortune, determining custody of the offspring, and dissolving the bonds of matrimony.

Jurisdiction Over the Person

The right to a day in court, the occasion to confront the witnesses testifying against you, representation by counsel, the opportunity to be heard: all of this and more goes into the Constitution's famous phrase, "due process of law." If you haven't thought much about "due process" since you had to memorize the Preamble in high school civics, remember that the Constitution guarantees that fair and just procedures will be adhered to in the judiciary. These fair and just procedures are required in *every* court.

Due process requires that before a person's rights and property are taken from him, he must be served with a summons so that he knows about the lawsuit and so that he may have the opportunity to present his side of the story. If your divorce suit asks for alimony, the house, the car, the checking account, or any of his other "property," and if you want custody of the children or any of his other "rights," you can't tell him you're having your hair done and secretly slip into the divorce court. The sheriff must serve your spouse with a summons, and your spouse must be given his "day in court."

If you want your divorce decree to affect your husband's rights (like visiting the children) or his property (as in payment of alimony), your husband must have his day in court, his opportunity to be heard, and this means he must be served with a summons that lets him know that a divorce suit was filed, what you claim he did wrong, what you are asking for, and when and where he can present his defense. Then, once your spouse has the summons, the court has *in personam* jurisdiction—that is, the judge can render a decree that affects his personal rights.

The usual way to get *in personam* jurisdiction is the sheriff's service of a summons on your spouse within the state in which you both live and where you filed your suit for divorce. Let's suppose, though, that your husband had moved out of the state. You'll have to pack your bag and sue him in the state where he is living in order to have *personal* jurisdiction over him. After all, the Constitution says that a man must have his day in court, so you can't sue an Oregon man in New Hampshire and expect him to come back East to defend. You want the divorce, the alimony, the child support—you go where he is.

The law understands, of course, that it may be a hardship to pack up and go to the place where an errant husband has set up housekeeping. After all, he lived with you in one state, and if he left you, it is his own fault that he's being sued for divorce. Realizing this, many states say that you can have *in personam* jurisdiction by having the summons served out of your state *if* he married you or was guilty of grounds *within* your state. These state laws say that the court has "long-arm" jurisdiction, to reach out and deal with the person who was in the state and then left. That is, once you've done something illegal in the state, you've subjected yourself to the possibility of being sued there so that crossing the state line in the hope of insulating yourself from being sued won't do much good. As long as you know where your husband has gone, he can be served with a summons and the court in the state where you live can give you a decree dissolving the marriage and affecting his *personal* rights.

Thus, it is possible to get an *in personam* divorce decree, a decree not only bringing about the dissolution of the marriage but also affecting his *personal* rights either by having him served with a summons in the state where you both live and where you filed for divorce, or by going off to the state where he is residing after he walked out, or, in states with long-arm laws, by suing him in the state where you both once lived after notifying him properly* even though he's found a new home elsewhere.

---

* State long-arm statutes specify precisely the notice that is required to subject an errant spouse to *in personam* jurisdiction. That notice may be by certified mail, with a published notice, etc.

Jurisdiction Over the Status of Marriage

Sociologists love to observe that the American people are rootless. They change climates and scenery, their companies transfer them, and many a wife spends a hefty percentage of her time wrapping her crystal in newspaper and unwrapping splintered glass. We are, indeed, a mobile people. And while most of the talk of mobility deals with *families* moving from place to place, there is plenty of moving where husbands (and, increasingly, wives) skip out on their families. Off they go, and often, no one knows where.

If the man you married has run and hasn't told you where he's gone, you obviously can't get personal jurisdiction over him, and due process of law forbids you to take away a man's property without letting him know. Again, the law makes allowances. It recognizes that husbands and wives do part and that they don't always send postcards or call home every Sunday when the rates are lower. Also, the law knows that it just isn't wise to believe that an abandoned spouse will sit by the window waiting for the other to return. You simply are not expected to celebrate your golden wedding anniversary a celibate. Life goes on, and so does divorce.

Once the court has jurisdiction over the status of the marriage, it can dissolve the marriage, but the judge will go no further. He will not grant alimony or determine custody without personal jurisdiction over the errant spouse. The only question is how does a court get jurisdiction over the status of the marriage and over the subject of *your* marriage in particular?

Every one of the fifty states looks upon its residents as its responsibility. You pay the taxes and the state sees that there are hospitals, schools, welfare payments, highways, and so forth. And while the state may not have received an invitation to your wedding, it did grant you the right to get married when it issued the license. Thus, although the state wasn't much help when your husband started staying out late at night, it is around to hear your story and dissolve the bonds of matrimony. So once you have taken up residence in a state, and maintained that residence for a year, or three years, or six weeks (depending on the state law), the courts of that state have jurisdiction over things that affect your personal status and that includes their having jurisdiction over the subject matter of your marriage.

For example, Alan and Mary marry and settle in Florida. Then Alan goes to Colorado on a business trip, falls for a stewardess en route and decides not to go home. In fact, he rents an apartment in Colorado. Now Mary is a resident of Florida. Florida has jurisdiction over her status, and she may file a suit for divorce in Florida. After mailing a notice to Alan at his last known address and publishing a notice in a local Florida newspaper, the Florida divorce court may dissolve the marriage. The Florida court has jurisdiction over the status of marriage (technically called *in rem* jurisdiction), but it does not have *in personam* jurisdiction over Alan. The Florida court can decree the divorce, but it cannot order Alan to pay for the children's upkeep. Likewise, if Alan stays in Colorado for the required period, Colorado has jurisdiction over his status. He may file his suit for divorce in Colorado, give Mary notice by mail, place an ad in a Colorado paper, and (assuming he has grounds) the Colorado court may dissolve his marriage. Again, though, the Colorado court has *in rem* jurisdiction only.

So it is possible to obtain a divorce based on *your* residence without having personal jurisdiction over your husband, but if you need an alimony order or an award of attorney's fees, or if you want a binding order that determines that you are entitled to child custody, you must bring your suit in a state that has jurisdiction *both* over your marriage (*in rem*) and over your husband (*in personam*).

The "Nevada" Divorce

Remember that spring afternoon when you lounged through your high school government class, and your teacher droned on about the "full faith and credit clause" of the Constitution? Well, even if you do remember what was said, you probably have forgotten entirely about Article 4, Section 1. That section provides that the court decrees of one state shall be given full faith and credit in every other state. That simply means that if a court in Iowa has jurisdiction over a case and hears the evidence and makes a decision, the courts of every other state of the union must accept the decision as valid, that is, give it full faith and credit. So, if you are divorced in one state, every other state must accept your divorce decree as valid—*if* the court that granted the divorce had jurisdiction over the subject matter of your marriage. Earlier you read that a state has jurisdiction over the status of marriage if one spouse has resided in the state for the statutory period of time. So does that mean you can pack up, fly to Las Vegas, stay in a motel the statutory six weeks, get a Nevada divorce, and come home again—free, with a divorce decree valid in your home state? No.

The state *issuing* a divorce may be satisfied that it has jurisdiction if a spouse has *resided* there for the time specified in its statute, but before the other states will accept the decree as valid and give the decree full faith and credit, they must be shown that the spouse was *domiciled* in the state that gave the decree. If you weren't *domiciled* in Nevada, your home state may not accept Nevada's jurisdiction and may set aside the decree.

If the distinction between *residence* and *domicile* and the whole question of when a decree will be granted full faith and credit sounds like the confusing product of attorneys' seminars, law journal articles, and Supreme Court decisions, you're absolutely correct.

To get us through the muddle, let's review the state's responsibility to its citizens. The people who make their home in a state can look to the state for services and protection and the state has the duty to look after its own. The law of the home state determines the status of its citizens—that is, whether a child is legally adopted, whether one is an heir and can inherit from a deceased second cousin who never got around to writing a will, and whether a person is single, married, or divorced. No state can make final, binding decisions affecting the status of a domiciliary of another state, even if that domiciliary resided within its borders.

The next logical question is: "What's the difference between a resident and a domiciliary?" A resident is someone who lives at a certain address: a domiciliary is a person who considers that address his home. A soldier can *reside* in Saigon, Vietnam, but Cedar Rapids, Iowa is his home—and it's Iowa law that determines questions of his personal status. A wife may stop over for six weeks in Reno, live out of a suitcase, and take a furnished room, but if she has a home in Arizona, if that's where she is registered to vote, if that's where she banks, and if her driver's license shows her address in Scottsdale, she's a domiciliary of Arizona. While Nevada may grant her a divorce, her husband can go to the courts in Arizona and they may refuse to recognize it.

Mr. and Mrs. S lived in Oregon, and Mrs. S filed her suit for divorce there. Her grounds were none too solid and after the judge heard the evidence, but before he actually decided the case, he wrote to the lawyers advising them that he was not convinced and that he was going to deny the divorce. The day after Mrs. S heard this, she left for Nevada. After six weeks there, she filed a suit for divorce there and won a decree. The decree was worthless according to the Oregon court. She was still married. It was clear that although Mrs. S had established a residence in Nevada, she never intended to remain there and was not a Nevada domiciliary. The decree was *not* accorded full faith and credit.

Of course, in order for a divorce decree to be set aside, someone has to contest it. If the divorced spouse says nothing, or if he shows up in the Nevada court (and, therefore, submits himself to the Nevada jurisdiction), or if he hears of the Nevada divorce and marries his secretary, there will be no contest as to whether or not the wife was an actual domiciliary of Nevada. The Nevada decree will be accorded full faith and credit; it will be valid in every other state.

If one morning you find that your husband has gone to Nevada for a six-week stay and you don't want a divorce: *see your lawyer.* If your husband should get the divorce decree, you can try to set it aside later, but an ounce of prevention may be your filing a "special" appearance in the Nevada court. By this procedure, you can fight out the question of whether he is really domiciled in Nevada, and, if you prove he's not, the Nevada court won't grant the decree at all. There are a couple of problems with this "special" appearance procedure. First, your lawyer must either go to Nevada or hire a Nevada lawyer to represent you, and this costs money. Second, if there's a trial in Nevada on the question of whether or not your husband is a domiciliary of that state, *you* may have to go to Nevada to testify. Third, you may lose. If the court finds that your husband is domiciled in Nevada, he can go ahead and seek the divorce and you'll have to defend or countersue for divorce in Nevada. If the divorce is granted, and you've fought out jurisdiction in Nevada, the decree will be accorded full faith and credit in every other state.

What to do when your husband flies to Nevada, then, and you don't want a divorce, is a complicated matter you must work out with your lawyer. Don't rush to Nevada; don't ignore the Nevada proceeding. *See your lawyer.*

One more word on the "Nevada" divorce. Remember that all the same provisions concerning jurisdiction apply. If the decree is entered on the basis of the plaintiff's residence in the state issuing the decree, and if there is no personal service of summons (no *in personam* jurisdiction over the defendant), the decree will be *in rem*. It will dissolve the bonds of matrimony, but it *cannot* affect the personal rights of the out-of-state defendant. This fact is clearly illustrated by the case of the Georgia housewife who got a Nevada divorce court to dissolve her marriage *and* to award her alimony to be paid every week. Back in Georgia her husband asked the Georgia court to set aside the Nevada decree. He won. The judge said, first, that he would not recognize the decree because although the housewife had been a resident of Nevada, she was domiciled in Georgia. Second, even if she had been domiciled in Nevada and the divorce itself were valid, the husband had never been served and no *in personam* order could be made against him—so the weekly alimony was improper because of lack of personal jurisdiction.

The moral of the story then is that if you want a divorce decree that is valid everywhere, sue where you are domiciled. And, if you want a divorce decree that goes further than simply dissolving the marriage, find your spouse and have him subjected to the jurisdiction of the court.

The "Mexican" Divorce

The "full faith and credit" clause of the Constitution requires that courts of every state are bound by the orders of other states when those states are exercising their jurisdiction. Why? All of the states are bound by the federal Constitution and the Bill of Rights so that we can be pretty certain that when a court in one state decides a case, it gave to the parties all of the rights guaranteed for fair trials. Most nations have the same ideas of due process of law and also have fair trials of the kind guaranteed in our Constitution. Occasionally, though, a nation takes a different view of justice. For example, during the Hitler regime, German laws blithely dispossessed the Jewish population of their property rights.

The U. S. courts refused to accept those laws or give such court decrees full faith and credit. And the United States courts didn't have to accept those decrees, because Article 4, Section 1, of the Constitution applies only to court proceedings of states of the Union.

When a foreign court proceeding is relied upon in a U. S. court, the court may review the record of the case. Only if it is satisfied that the case met constitutional standards of fairness will it accept the decree of the foreign court. This is called "comity," or the mutual friendship and respect between nations of the world. If the U.S. courts see in the record of a foreign case that something is amiss, particularly from the standpoint of due process of law, they can toss the foreign decree into the nearest wastebasket and start all over again. Foreign divorce decrees have found their way to the junk heap on occasions when the "divorced" spouse tries to rely on a foreign decree to collect alimony, child support, or to press other rights granted in the decree.

Any foreign decree will be scrutinized before a U.S. court accepts it. Just as in divorces involving different states, the courts look first at jurisdiction. The U.S. courts are far more likely to accept the validity of a foreign decree when the plaintiff was truly domiciled in the foreign country that rendered the divorce. The question is then: "Was the plaintiff who received the divorce domiciled in the other nation, or did he go there just to take advantage of easy divorce laws?" If domicile is genuine, the divorce usually will be accepted. However, if the plaintiff is domiciled in the foreign nation, unless her spouse is served according to due process, she can obtain only an *in rem* divorce. Again, the rights of the defendant to his property cannot be interfered with unless the court has *in personam* jurisdiction. The person being sued must have legal notice of the case and an opportunity to defend and tell his side of the story.

When we talk about the validity of foreign divorces, we

almost always think of the "old days"—the days, a few years ago, when Mexico was a haven for the quicky divorce. It was possible to cross the border, see a bullfight, unload your spouse, and head north again. Sometimes, Mexican courts granted divorces by mail. However, in the last few years, Mexico has abandoned the laws allowing for "quicky" divorces.

Mr. C had a girl friend whom he was crazy about, but Mrs. C didn't share his enthusiasm for separation. She refused to divorce her husband. He and his girl ran off to Mexico. He got a divorce, married his girl friend, and went back home. Mrs. C went to court. The Mexican decree was absolutely void, because Mr. C was neither a domiciliary nor a resident of Mexico. His second "marriage" was bigamous and void.

In another case, a New Jersey man and his wife were at odds. He had a girl on the side but kept his "friendship" with her a secret from his wife, fearing that she would seek a bundle of alimony if she sued for divorce on the grounds of adultery. He thought, unwisely, that he could fly to Mexico, get a divorce without alimony, and marry his sweetheart. And he did. But his first wife went to the New Jersey Court of Chancery, which held that the husband had never been domiciled in Mexico but had gone there, indeed, only to evade his duties under New Jersey law. The second marriage was declared bigamous and void. Wife number one then sued for divorce on the grounds of her husband's adultery, pointing to the weekend trip south of the border, and won a New Jersey divorce and alimony, too.

In a twist on an old story, Mr. and Mrs. B were married after Mr. B secretly had obtained a mail-order Mexican divorce from his first wife. Mr. B and his second wife lived together and had four children. Then things began to sour. In a violent argument, Mr. B blurted out the facts of his first marriage and his mail-order foreign divorce that had made their marriage possible, and *she* filed suit for divorce. She claimed that Mr. B's first marriage was still alive and well because the foreign divorce was invalid. She argued that she was the innocent victim of her husband's bigamy—and she won a divorce.

Again, as in divorces in this country, the foreign decree will stand as valid until someone comes along to contest it. One man took his kids off to play tennis at a park near his home in Washington, D.C. He left the children at the tennis court, slipped through the locker room, and went off for a three-week vacation to Mexico, during which he divorced his wife and married his travelling companion. When he returned, his D.C. wife was delighted to be divorced, but she wanted and needed child support. She filed a suit in the District of Columbia, refusing to contest the validity of the Mexican decree, but asking only that her former husband be ordered to pay support. The judge looked at the Mexican decree, accepted it (no one gave him any reasons to do otherwise, and for all he knew, the husband had been validly domiciled in Mexico for years), but did order the husband to pay child support. Again, the trip to Mexico to avoid the obligations of laws the states impose was a total flop.

Thus the best course of action is to sue for divorce where you are domiciled and preferably where your spouse can be served with a summons. Divorces present enough problems. Having your decree set aside and having to do the whole thing all over again is too much for anyone.

19

Child Custody

Just as the beasts of field and forest will fight to protect their own, so the male human will ferociously defend his right to custody of—his car. Against the onslaughts of divorce proceedings, husbands violently fend off all efforts to deprive them of exclusive control of their three-speed, automatic-change, stereophonic, tapedeck-cartridge-cassette-recorder, with headphones and simulated genuine alligator carrying case. Yet these same men will ordinarily turn child custody over to their wives without a whimper. And since most women want custody, this may be the only issue on which divorcing spouses agree.

In the property settlement agreement and the divorce decree, the paragraph on child custody will usually give you the "exclusive care, custody, control, and education" of your children. In other words, the decisions that married parents usually reach together are now the decisions of the parent who has custody. You decide when your daughter may wear lipstick and whether your son wears shorts, knickers, or long pants. How late they watch TV, and whether Little League is a good idea, are matters you must now work out on your own. You choose the dentist, the pediatrician, and the summer camp. You choose the neighborhood and the neighbors, the religious education or lack of it.

There are only a few factors that tend to limit your *"exclusive* care, custody, control, and education" of the children. One, of course, is money, and we'll see what their father's duties are in that regard later on. Other factors may be written into the property settlement agreement or decree itself. For example, if you know dad is coming to visit, you can't stow the children out of sight when he comes around to pick them up. If the agreement is to send the children to their father's church for Sunday School, you'd better get them up, get them dressed, and get them there on Sunday mornings. Then, too, common sense will tell you that while your ex may be a jerk to you, he's still "daddy" to your children, and tough as it may seem, you must try to get along with as little friction as possible on the one thing that still holds you together—your children. And, finally, the most important limitation on how you exercise custody is that you keep first and foremost the best interests of your children. Love, concern, and the opinions of others may motivate married people in the way they care for their children. As a divorced parent, add to those that child custody has become a privilege that you can lose if the judge becomes convinced that the best interests of your kids call for a change. But, it's a little too soon here to talk about *changes* in child custody and so we'll cover this subject in detail later on.

Now it shouldn't surprise you that fathers are usually so willing to turn over their children's custody—(and their children's good-night kisses, their grammar school potluck dinners, their temper tantrums, and mumps and stomachaches). After all, if he were truly a devoted father, the odds are you wouldn't be getting a divorce in the first place. Every so often, a man will contest your having custody; should this be part of your divorce case, it's the nastiest, messiest, and most heartbreaking part of all. Let's look into that possibility and see what's involved.

First, let's recognize that some men will threaten to fight over child custody to chew you down on alimony. You and your lawyer will be able to appraise the sincerity of his threat and how to handle it. Of course, a threat like this never should be taken lightly. Second, a husband may truly want to have his children with him. Third (it's difficult, but face it), your husband may sincerely believe that you are not a fit mother.

When custody is contested, there is a trial. Your lawyer will present all of the evidence he can to show that the children should live with you. Your husband's lawyer will present his side of the case. The judge will look at you, your appearance, and how you conduct yourself. He'll listen to witnesses, usually neighbors or teachers who know you and your children. Occasionally, the children will talk to a psychiatrist who may testify, and sometimes the judge will invite the children into his chambers and try to get to know them. The judge will take into account the child's age, sex, and health. Sometimes, the state will investigate and file a report. Like any other law case, the trial may last for one hour or several days. There may be one witness or many. Just how the custody hearing is conducted is in your lawyer's hands. The judge will listen to all of the facts and then apply the rules of law to them and decide the case.

Most of our rules of law have their beginnings in early English traditions—what we call the common law. In merry old England, the children were apprenticed, working and earning their way at seven or eight years old. The parent who had custody was entitled to keep all of the money that the little ones earned. So, under the early common law, the father was almost always given custody—and he got his cut of the profits. As time went on, the children stayed home with mother and the courts went in the opposite direction. Unless she was an absolute beast, mom got custody. Today, thanks (or no thanks) to Sigmund Freud and woman's lib, the judges are looking more and more into the facts of each family situation. They still favor the mother, and she has the better chance of receiving custody, but the rule of law now is that custody will be given to the parent who will see to the child's best interests, whichever parent that may be.

A few years ago, the Supreme Court of Iowa had to decide which parent should win custody of two children. The judges observed that, in most custody cases, the mother usually gets custody because she does the household duties and devotes more of her time to the children. But, in the case they decided, both mom and dad had always worked. It wasn't the old question of staying either with mom or with dad's housekeeper. The facts showed that both parents were fit, but that the father spent far more time caring for the children. As a result, the Supreme Court judges thought that the father was a better parent than the mother and awarded him custody.

Judges have a terrible time deciding custody cases and now and then will try a King Solomon tactic. They split the baby down the middle with something lawyers call "split custody." That's six months with dad and six months with mom—but since split custody might result in split personality, this "solution" is mercifully rare. And there's another unwise King Solomon split. It goes like this: the girls to the mother, the boys to the father; or a variation—the toddlers to mom, the teen-agers to dad. Again, it's mercifully rare.

The phrase "unfit mother" brings to mind a painted hussy leaning against a lamppost wearing a satin skirt and feather boa. But a mother also may be unfit in the sense that she is unable to care for a child. Serious physical or mental illness, alcoholism, or drug addiction may make one unfit. Women have lost custody because of emotional instability, several prior divorces, or evidence that they neglected their children. Mr. S has custody of the child his wife abandoned on the church steps. An Arizona man fought to prove his wife unfit because she was a member of the Jehovah's Witnesses. The child was not allowed to pledge allegiance to the flag in school and his father believed that, in time, his son would be teased and criticized. The court agreed that being different may cause ridicule, but may strengthen a character as well. The judges said that religious difference did not make the mother unfit. Of course, if you're thinking of teaching your child the joys of burning witches at the stake, you might be ruled unfit.

What if your husband sues *you* for divorce? If he proves that he's right and you're wrong, will the court give him custody of the children? Fortunately, custody is not taken away to punish a guilty parent. It is the child's welfare that is considered. So a good mother usually gets custody.

But there *is* a catch. Some judges don't believe a woman can be a good mother if she is guilty of grounds for divorce. The statute in Alabama says that any woman who would abandon her husband is automatically denied custody of her school-age children. And many judges believe that any woman who would sleep with another man must be unfit. A woman found to have had a love affair lost custody, alimony, attorney's fees, and was sent into the world with only "her clothing and personal ornaments." Old England again? Not at all—1967, Nebraska. And one judge became so incensed over a woman's peccadilloes that he questioned her, asked her if she slept naked, called her a "tramp," and, for a finale, quoted from the Ten Commandments. Did she lose her custody battle during the Victorian era? No—1965, Washington, D.C.

Yet the trend seems to be to the realization that women, like men, sometimes slip, and this doesn't automatically make them a Sadie Thompson or the Wicked Witch of the West where their children are concerned. If it's your habit to entertain a variety of gents, or if you're about as easy to get as a cutrate hooker with a past-due charge account at Saks, you're running a risk.

You must realize by now that a custody contest can provide enough gossip to light up a small-town switchboard for days. While people are married, they have complete charge of their children, and, unless the kids play hookey, or are undernourished, or seriously abused, Big Brother is not watching. Get a divorce and fight over custody, and the state enters the scene. Now it will sift through the evidence (and the dirty laundry) because the children must be protected. Occasionally, the court finds neither parent is fit—then what? Two teen-agers married, became parents, and divorced. These kids were more concerned with clearing up their acne than tending to their offspring, so the court gave custody to the grandparents. In another case, the grandpa had plenty of money and all the luxuries to offer his grandchildren, but he could not give them what their mother could—they stayed with her.

Mrs. V committed adultery, Mr. V was a mental and physical wreck, and grandma and grandpa were aged and not too stable either. With a choice like that, a little adultery doesn't seem half bad. Mrs. V kept her children.

Where things are really bad, the judge has a last resort. He may place the children with a state agency. If neither parent shapes up, the children may even be adopted as if they were orphans. In each instance, the law is trying to do the best it can for the child. But can you explain this case? After reviewing all the facts, the state Supreme Court declared that both spouses cheated and both were unfit parents. What to do with the four children? Well, two of them went with unfit dad, and two of them with unfit mom. That's a double-decker divorce case—a break-up of husband and wife and of sisters and brothers, too.

Here we are bouncing junior back and forth like a ping-pong ball. Doesn't he have anything to say about where he'll live? Can you lose him to his father's bribe of a ten-speed, hand-braked, lambskin-seated English racer bike? Will he go home to papa if sonny can't watch the late late show and finger-paint the living room walls?

The state of Utah thought it was only fair to give children of ten years and older the right to select the parent who would be awarded custody. When mom and dad got a divorce in Utah, their fifth-grader had them in the palm of his hand. One could see a trend of power-crazed, brown-shirted ten-year-olds goose-stepping around the backyard shrieking "Tomorrow, the world!" In 1969, the Utah legislature repealed the statute. This is not to say that the children's wishes are completely ignored. Teen-agers' preferences based on fair reasoning are often followed by the judge. A sixteen-year-old South Carolinian chose his adoptive father over his natural mother and the court agreed. A Louisiana judge wanted to deprive Mrs. P of custody after her husband's detectives surprised her in bed with her beau, but her seventeen- and eighteen-year-old children were more tolerant. They preferred mom to dad and the judge gave in. After all, as a practical matter, how could the judge enforce a custody order against the wishes of two near-adults? When Mr. and Mrs. K went to divorce court, their boy, age 12, chose to live with his dad. He told the judge that dad would help him with arithmetic, never disciplined him, and, in general, was more fun. The judge wasn't impressed with this grade-school logic, and custody of junior was awarded to Mrs. K.

Finally, it must be said that a child custody contest can be even more upsetting to the child than to the parents. Avoid this battle if you can, but don't plan on giving in now and fighting for custody later. Children shouldn't be shuttled back and forth from dad's house to mom's house, and the judges know it. You love your children and so you should approach the question of their custody with at least the wisdom of the law. Think of what is best for your child—then make it happen.

20

Visitation

A parent who doesn't have custody still has the right to see the children. This right is called "visitation" (the word makes me think of open house at the county jail). No, he doesn't look longingly at his offspring through a wire screen; instead, he looks longingly at his offspring while they bowl together on a Sunday afternoon. Visitation is not only a right of the parent, it's considered to be healthy for the children. If you have child custody, you must allow visitation; only an occasional mass-murderer is denied this right. Don't be surprised if their father exercises his visitation rights. He may have ignored the kids when you were married, but the zoos, museums, and miniature golf courses are filled every weekend with bored men trying to prove to themselves and the world that they are good fathers after all.

When and Where
Visitation may be every Sunday, every other Wednesday,

one weekend a month, two weeks during summer vacation, Thanksgiving, President Harding's birthday, Maundy Thursday, all or none of the above. Usually visitation will be one day each week. When visitation will occur is a detail that your lawyer will work out in the property settlement agreement. But keep in mind that if you don't agree to something, the judge will order visitation anyway.

Visitation is reserved for the noncustodial parent. It's rare that a court will order visitation by others—like your in-laws, for example. You don't have to reserve another visiting day for his side of the family, unless, of course, you've said that you would in the property settlement agreement or the judge has ordered it. Often, your husband's day will be spent partly with his family; that's fine and his prerogative. But, whatever you do, remember that when the property settlement agreement or order doesn't govern your decisions, it's the welfare of the children that does. It may be that the children have a deep affection for their paternal grandparents. If they don't see them on visiting day, call and arrange an afternoon with grandpa. Your divorcing their son needn't mean that your children "divorce" their grandparents.

The Irresponsible Visitor

Visitation is a day with dad away from your home and your watchful eye. Unless he's visiting an infant, he has the right to take the child out of the home.

If your ex is likely to perch the kids on the bar in the local pub while he has a few, or if he might bring them home at midnight, tell your lawyer. He'll write in the agreement that visitation shall be on such and such a day "during daylight hours" or "from 10:00 A.M. to 6:00 P.M." He'll tell your husband's lawyer that if dad abuses his visitation privilege, the judge will be advised. It is unlikely that a judge will deny all rights of visitation, but he may dole out a lecture in the courtroom and suspend the right for a while, or he may limit visitation to a few supervised and chaperoned hours at a time.

If You Plan to Move

When you broke up with your high school "steady," you gave back his letter sweater and class ring, and it was good-bye. When childless couples divorce, they, too, may go their separate ways. But this is not the case if you have children. On the morning of every visiting day, you may see his smiling countenance, or at least hear his car drive up. When they come home, your kids will tell you what daddy's doing and what daddy said, and how clever daddy is. Grin and bear it. So long as he wants to see them, you can't run away—or can you?

At the beginning of this book, we said that there are three parties to every divorce case, you, he, and the state. Also, the court that grants the divorce has "continuing jurisdiction," so that the same court can always make orders for support, alimony, and so forth, on into the future. If there are no children, you are free to come and go as you please, from state to state, nation to nation. But, if you have children, then you stay under the state's thumb until they are grown. The judges are "uncles" who look over your shoulder to be sure that your offspring are being well cared for. If dad doesn't pay his child support, you tell "uncle" and dad may be punished. If "uncle" says their father will see the kids every other Tuesday—they'd better be available, or "uncle" may punish you.

Does this mean that Our Gal Sunday may never leave the mining town? No. It means that she must ask permission first. Mrs. S was divorced in Washington State. Every week Mr. S strolled up her front walk for his visitation rights and every week Mrs. S became more and more infuriated. Finally, she packed up her bags, took the kids, and went East. She didn't say "May I?" The court in Washington said that any woman who would run away from a court order giving visitation has no respect for the law and must be an unfit mother. She lost custody of the children. Mrs. D took the children all the way to West Germany. It took Mr. D almost three years to complain. He didn't seem like a red-hot father, so there was no change in custody. But Mrs. D was in contempt of court for leaving the state without permission, and the judge could have sent her on an all-expense-paid trip to jail.

Sure, you and the kids can take a vacation and the kids can go to summer camp, but if you plan to move out of the state as soon as the divorce is final, say it in the property settlement agreement. Get approval in the divorce decree* and arrange visitation with the distances in mind. For example, instead of visitation every Sunday, he may see the children one weekend a month and several weeks over summer vacation.

Your Attitude

In the heat of your divorce case, this may seem like advice that's impossible to follow—but, on the subject of visitation, be friendly! Be sure that the kids are available for Father's Day; if he's crazy about trees, arrange visitation for Arbor Day. Remember, your birthday may fall on "his" Sunday— if you're flexible, chances are he will be. If he has tickets for the World Series, for heaven's sake, let the kids go with him.

When they go off with dad, encourage the offspring to put smiles on their scrubbed faces. You may not be able to force your teen-agers to spend Sunday with their dad when their friends are all at the beach, but you surely can cajole the little ones to look forward to visiting on Sunday.

The temptation is there for you to criticize your ex during the week. Remember, he'll find out about that on visiting

---

*Changes in visitation and how to make them *after* the property settlement agreement and divorce decree are discussed in chapter twenty-six.

day. And remember, too, that it's best for your children that they love, like, and respect their father. Let them enjoy their Sundays—and even their Sunday evenings when they come home. Fight the urge to put your kids to the third degree as soon as they cross the threshold. What they ate—where they went—did daddy yell at them—was daddy with a lady—was she pretty? Relax. The story of Sunday will unfold during the week anyway, and you don't want your children to train for a career with the CIA by spying on dad—or you. If he spends visiting day telling the kids how miserable you are, just take it easy. Their loyalty will be with you and his backbiting will only backfire.

Enjoy your day off. Visiting day is his day with the children and your day to shop, read, see a movie, or take a nap. Just think of it—a day to yourself and no babysitter to pay.

21

The Child Support
Allowance

NOTHING is too good for your child. Heifetz should teach him violin and Nureyev should visit weekly to watch your daughter's arabesque. The little ones should trip off to school outfitted by Florence Eisemann, enjoy riding in summer, Alpine skiing in winter, visit Dr. Salk for their polio shots, and have Dr. Bettelheim to babysit. But who is going to pay for all this? Who is going to pay for the school bus, the sneakers, lunch in the cafeteria, crayons ranging from puce to burnt sienna, calamine lotion, and guitar lessons. Who? None other than that wonderful man who had the "pro" check his golf swing, but wouldn't hire a plumber to make the toilet flush; who couldn't afford the opera, but who had box seats at the football game. Yes—that same generous guy who bought you an iron for your birthday.

The Child Support Obligation
If you have custody of the children, their father should

send you an allowance to support them. The law is that a father has an obligation to support his offspring. Yet, while you'd have a difficult time convincing some men of it, the setting of a child support allowance is a *benefit* to the parent who has to pay it. Here's why. The law says that a parent is financially responsible for his child's "necessaries." This means that a child's clothing bills, education expenses, housing, medical attention, and so forth can be charged to his dad. You go to a department store and charge junior's snowsuit and galoshes and the department store can turn around and collect from junior's father. Your daughter sprains her ankle at the playground and the doctor who puts the bandage on it can collect his fee from your husband. But, once a property settlement agreement and divorce decree say dad's obligation is, for example, $20.00 a week, that's the extent of it. That's where his responsibility stops. Once he's paid his $20.00 a week, he's done his duty and if your charge account shows $40.00 a week for your offspring's school clothes, you'd better have the extra $20.00 to pay it.

If you're a strong-willed, independent lady, you may be tempted to say, "I have custody and I'll support my baby myself. I don't want a dime from that no good ‡*%‡*‡." Don't be too surprised if the judge insists that you put some figure in the divorce decree and call it child support. If your folks left you acres of oil wells and your husband can barely afford oil for his Honda, you will still be required to put a child support figure in the property settlement agreement and divorce decree. Why? If not to help you—then to help him. If the child support award is $1.00 a month—then that's the extent of his child support obligation and the orthodontist, pediatrician, and tutor will not be able to collect more from him.

Since a father has a legal obligation to support his children, the first question that must blushingly be answered is: "Are the children his?" This question shouldn't be a toughy, but if it is, the rule of law will help you. The law is that children born during marriage are presumed legitimate. The judges dislike declaring children bastards and will bend over backwards to declare a child the offspring of married parents. This is the rule even if he wins a divorce on the grounds of your adultery. Don't charge your husband with impotency though, and then ask him to support your kid. Five months after a GI returned from the army, his wife presented him with a robust and healthy baby. He presented her with a divorce and no child support. But if you were a little bit pregnant when he married you, the child is presumed to be his, and where Mr. and Mrs. M married just after the baby was born, the judge decided Mr. M had done the "right" thing and was the father.

There are two ways a man can become a father: the usual way and by adoption. An adoptive father is just like a natural father so far as custody and support are concerned. If you had children when he married you, and he adopted them, he is obliged to support them. "Adoption" means the legal proceeding, not just letting the kids use his name or his treating them as if they were his own. Your children from a prior marriage, if they aren't adopted, are not your present husband's obligation. He doesn't owe a nickel of child support for them, even if you've all been supported by him during your marriage. An Idaho woman had four children, and after her divorce, their father disappeared. Still attractive, and lucky, she remarried and her second husband took care of her and the four children, and ultimately another child, born of the second marriage. But when they divorced, she was on her own again with the first four children. The Idaho Supreme Court recognized that the woman and her brood would be destitute and decided that the youngest child should have the nice things his father could provide, so custody of the youngest went to dad.

Lest Betty Friedan, Kate Millett, and Gloria Steinem

misunderstand, let me be clear. Child support is an obligation of *both* husband and wife. When the judge decides "how much," he looks at *both* incomes. A working woman is likely to supplement her former husband's child support. For example, when the mother has custody and works part-time, the father may get a reduction. The way it usually works is that a man's salary that was just adequate to support his family when he was married will shrink when it must pay for alimony, child support, and for his separate apartment, telephone, and other expenses. Even getting one-half of his income in child support and alimony may not be enough to meet your normal expenses. Once you polish up your shorthand skills or revalidate your teaching certificate and start receiving a salary, you, too, are capable of contributing to child support. And with a low bow and doff of the hat to equality—where both mom and dad work and dad has custody—the courts have often ordered mom to make child support payments.

The Child Support Allowance—How Much?

Now I know you're asking "how much?" child support allowance, and I wish I could set up a neat chart so that you would know exactly where you stand. Unfortunately, the slide rule hasn't been invented that takes into account the factors that might be considered. Here's what's involved: your husband's income, your income, the number of children, their ages, his health, your health, the kids' health, your standard of living before the divorce, you, your husband's, and your children's special skills, needs, and disabilities. Add to these the important intangibles of your lawyer's skill in negotiating the property settlement agreement, or in a case in which you are unable to agree, the judge's philosophy and experience. And while most judges say that when it comes to child support, they won't consider who is guilty of grounds for divorce, a real stinker may get nipped worse than an innocent victim.

What about Joe Generous who keenly feels his obligation to support himself with life's necessities, like a cashmere sport jacket, alligator shoes, and a dime-thin wrist watch, but tells you that if you want more than $5.00 a week in child support, he'll simply quit his job? First, he's probably bluffing. After all, if he quits, who'll keep up the payments on his air-conditioned convertible? Second, the law won't let him get away with it. Remember, parents have an obligation to support their offspring—and generally, at a standard of living similar to the one the children had before their parents' divorce.

One dentist had drilled teeth at the rate of $50,000 a year and decided that rather than pay child support, he would golf Mondays, Wednesdays, and Fridays. The judge sent him right back to his baby blue drill and piped-in music by fixing child support on the basis of a $50,000 a year income. Another man claimed that an injury to his finger made it impossible for him to continue his work as a skilled watchmaker. The judge informed him that duty to his kids must come before professional pride and suggested he get a job, any job, and fast. Mr. and Mrs. R and their children lived at the brink of poverty on the meager wages he brought home now and then when he felt like doing a day's work. When they divorced, the judge set the child support allowance at a figure to provide moderately, but decently for the kids and directed Mr. R to pay it—even if it meant that he find regular work! Then there was the man who was everyone's good neighbor, a really great guy. He volunteered for church work, he ran a Boy Scout pack, he was always around when anyone needed a helping hand. That is, anyone but his children. So busy was he that he only had time to work a few days a week. But the judge taught him that charity begins at home.

Remember, if you have custody and if child support is set in the divorce decree, you aren't stuck with that amount. It can be upped (or decreased) by later court proceedings and we'll get into the hows and whys when we talk about changes after the divorce decree in chapter twenty-six. However, there's nothing to prevent you from making informal changes from time to time. For example, your daughter wins the school science fair award with a rare display of mold scraped off of the cream cheese you forgot to throw away. She can enter her mold in the competition at the state fair—but the train ride and hotel will put a squeeze on your budget. For heaven's sake, ask dad to pay for it. Wheedle, cajole, write him a sweet note, mention it when he stops by to visit. You've got nothing to lose and he may just want to brag about his daughter's blue ribbon. Give him the opportunity to "volunteer" these little extras. And if he pays his daughter's transportation, odds are, he'll even up and buy his son's catcher's mitt. If your ex finds that he can blow $100 on a girl he picked up, he may be perfectly willing—and even delighted—to pay for day camp, a special party dress, or membership at the "Y." He may absolutely turn you down on Monday when you ask for school bus money and happily write out a check on Tuesday to pay for ballet slippers, matching tutu, and leotard. He may be motivated by love or guilt or generosity. He may be showing off, taking the credit, or reminding the kids what a great guy he is. Enjoy it!

How and When It's Paid and Who Receives It

The property settlement agreement and divorce decree should be specific about when child support is paid. He must pay on the first of the month, every Tuesday, or some other set arrangement. If your ex usually gets paid on Saturday, it's a good idea to have the child support payment due every Saturday. A man who was irresponsible about money before your divorce isn't about to change and if he's the last of the big-time spenders, have him pay you weekly instead of monthly so he doesn't have to write a big check with what may be a little balance.

Once you've agreed on the amount, be sure that you are going to get all of it by checking the arithmetic. If he is to pay $50.00 a week—that's *not* $200 a month. There are usually more than four weeks in a month, you know. Only a few days? Well, add it up and see if it matters at the end of the year:

$$\begin{array}{ccc}
\$\ \ 50 & & \$\ \ 200 \\
\times\ \underline{\ \ 52}\text{ weeks} & or & \times\ \underline{\ \ 12}\text{ months} \\
\$2,600 & & \$2,400
\end{array}$$

That $200 difference will pay for plenty of peanut butter, so be careful. What if the first week he pays you on Monday, the second week Tuesday, the third week, Wednesday, and so on? This arrangement is okay, just be sure that he pays you *every* week.

Go out and buy yourself a notebook and keep a record of when he pays child support and how much. This is particularly helpful if he was an expert cheater at Monopoly and kept the score in his favor when you played Scrabble. Even if he's not sneaky, you'll want the notebook if he's inclined to pay in irregular amounts. The notebook will help your lawyer in court if your ex stops paying. The book may help out on your income tax records, too.*

Sometimes the child support payments will be ordered to be sent directly to your son's military school, or to the bank that has the mortgage on the house you live in. The general rule is that child support is paid to the parent who has custody. When we talked about child custody, we said that custody usually means the right to decide on the schools, house, diet, and so forth of the child. So you receive the

---

* Income tax is discussed in chapter twenty-three.

allowance and you spend it as you see fit, remembering always that the child's welfare comes first. You're bound to mix up the child support payments, your alimony, salary, etc., in one bank account or sugar bowl and that's okay, but having your hair tipped with the last of the milk money is *not* a good idea.

Duration of the Allowance

The child support allowance, like all good things, comes to an end. You had better not rely on it to furnish you with life's niceties and old age retirement. The allowance is, after all, to protect children, and while your 6'2", 180-pound son may still be "baby" to you, he may be on his own so far as the law is concerned. The parents' legal duty to support a child ends when he reaches "majority" or is "emancipated." In most states, "majority" comes sometime between the eighteenth and twenty-first birthdays. Emancipation happens when a kid is considered to be on his own, even if he isn't old enough to drink or vote. So, if your sixteen-year-old runs off and gets married (heaven forbid!) she's on her own—and no child support. If your boy quits high school to join the Marine Corps, your husband is off the hook for the child support.

If you have a child who is physically or mentally unable to take care of himself, and will probably remain so even after he is technically no longer a minor, tell your lawyer. The father's duty of support may end when that child reaches majority, unless you have specifically provided for support beyond that time. Fathers have been ordered to support their adult, but disabled offspring, but some courts still adhere to the old rule that when a child is "of age," support ends. Settling this question in the property settlement agreement may save both heartache and hardship later.

When your son's first-grade teacher tells you that junior "talks back," do you envision him as a leading lawyer speaking out for the rights of the downtrodden? When he experimented by combining your hand lotion and perfume in the Tupperware, could you see him as "my son, the dermatologist"? You may be concerned today with getting him through the third grade, but your property settlement agreement looks to tomorrow, so try to arrange for child support allowance payments to continue through college education. University tuition, books, housing, lab fees, and football tickets are problems for married parents, but a divorced woman whose child support may end at high school graduation had better plan now. The latest trend in the courts is that a child who is worthy of college should have his chance, and a father's obligation for child support may be ordered extended through the college years. But you can't be sure that a judge will consider your little angel college material—particularly if his high school average is less than straight A; and you can never be certain what the court trend will be years from now when all of his friends are sending away for university catalogs. Best to arrange for this in the property settlement agreement and divorce decree now.

You want the best for your children and so should their father. If he has cheerfully passed to you the responsibilities of caring for the children, he should be inconvenienced at least to the extent of properly supporting them. Hopefully, support should be enough so that the children can stay in the same neighborhood, attend the same school, and have the birthday parties, lessons, and other extra treats they enjoyed before the divorce, and hopefully, their father will want to guarantee these for his children. The economic realities may make total continuity impossible, but work it out with your lawyer and listen to what he tells you. The husband who thinks that divorce means that he can pamper himself and walk away from his duty to his children may yet be taught to grow up.

22

Alimony

Alimony, say it slowly. Let the word roll off
your tongue, Al-i-mo-ny. Now count backwards from 100
and dream of Hollywood, of heart-shaped swimming pools,
pink mink, diamond pendants, rings, tiaras, brooches. Got
the idea? Well, unless you're a movie queen with an oil-rich
husband, forget it.

For all the magic of the word, for all the fabulous tabloid
stories, alimony is simply an allowance to pay for the support
of a spouse unable to provide for herself after the marriage
is washed up. Alimony isn't an automatic benefit. Unlike
child support, which a father *must* pay, alimony is decreed
only under certain circumstances. It can be waived, denied,
and forgotten. Sometimes, the court decrees so little that it's
forgettable. Alimony most resembles a pension. After years
of faithful service, dishpan hands, housemaid's knee, and the
stimulating career of folding T-shirts warm from the dryer,
the wife (whose husband has found a young thing with

ivory hands, unknobbed knees, and a French hand laundry) is given a stipend to get her through old age. What the gold watch and profit-sharing fund are to the corporation's bookkeeper, alimony is to the abandoned housewife.

When Alimony Is Denied

The woman who, under sound mind, disposing memory and free from threats from her dear husband, gives up the right to claim alimony will never get a second chance at it. Once waived, alimony is gone forever. So, when the noble spirit moves you, take a cold shower and a quick jog around the block. Imagine yourself as aged, with skin crinkly as tissue paper, and hanging over the windowsill waiting for the mailman to bring your Social Security check. If you still plan to waive alimony, you are either noble, independently wealthy, loaded with foolish pride, or so guilty of grounds for divorce yourself that you're willing to trade in your alimony for a divorce decree. My advice is this: Be noble if you must; give up your alimony without giving up your right to try for it later if things get tough (and *he* gets rich). Reserving alimony of even as little as $1.00 a year will allow you to keep your pride, and yet it is not a waiver so that you still may apply for a larger amount later.

Courts will refuse to award alimony to the wife whose marriage was little longer than a leisurely honeymoon. Today's judges are denying alimony to women whose marriage has neither interrupted their education nor their career. While many judges won't hire women lawyers, pay salaries to their women clerks commensurate with the men, or let women join their professional societies, they have become stout adherents to woman's lib where alimony is concerned.

Many states consider alimony a reward for services rendered and earned only by the ideal little woman. Regardless of the length of the marriage and the years spent at the kitchen sink and away from the job market, if the wife slips and is found guilty of grounds for divorce, she will be denied alimony. This position explains why it's better to sue for divorce than be sued. If you are sued, you'll get the same divorce from the bonds of matrimony, but that may be all you get. One woman was denied alimony because of her "offensive behavior" in that she used "coarse and indelicate language." Another woman wrote anonymous letters slandering her husband and his daughter, and she, too, was denied alimony. The Virginia Supreme Court of Appeals declared only a few years ago that a woman has no right to alimony if her husband wins a divorce because of her misconduct, and the statute in Louisiana requires that the judge conclude that the wife "has not been at fault" before he has the right to give her alimony. In both Michigan and Florida, a wife may receive alimony even if she was not blameless, but fie upon the "adulteress." No matter how long she's been married or how destitute she may be, if found guilty of committing adultery, the courts of those two states will send her naked into the world.

The view that I prefer, and so I'll call it the "modern and enlightened view," is that fault is only one of many factors to be considered in determining whether alimony should be granted and how much. It is, after all, a myth (which the divorce law perpetuates as gospel) that one party has the blame for a marriage gone bad, and the other is the innocent victim. It should be accepted that both parties contribute to the divorce (but often in different degrees).

Many courts have declared that comparative guilt of the parties is only one of many considerations in determining the grant or denial of alimony. A Minnesota woman misbehaved, but only after twenty-three years of marriage. She was middle-aged, without vocational skills or prospects of employment. She received her stipend. Another "guilty" woman was given alimony after the judge decided that she had neither income nor assets. A wife charged and found guilty of cruelty to her husband was allowed alimony equal to the amount of cash she contributed to buy their home.

Thus, it can be said that alimony may be denied where it is waived, where it is not needed, and where it has not been earned by the leading of a blameless life.

Determining the Amount of Alimony

Behind a handsome alimony award, there may be lurking a skilled trial lawyer and a clever negotiator. Most often the amount of alimony awarded is not arrived at by the judge listening to evidence of the husband's income and the wife's needs, but rather by his lawyer and hers haggling in an office, over the phone, in the corridors of the courthouse, or even in the judge's chambers. Whether the attorneys arrive at the figure and the judge approves it, or the judge initially fixes the alimony, there are certain facts that must be taken into account. The first is the financial status of the parties.

Contrary to your wildest fantasies, there is no way that a woman will get alimony of $50,000 from a man worth $10,000. So the initial question is: "What is the husband worth?" If the husband crept into an early retirement when the divorce suit was filed, the judge will take into account what he should be earning. The award of alimony may return a wage earner from the tennis courts to his desk.

Future income is also considered. Mrs. T worked as a secretary so that Mr. T could complete his education. Her salary paid his tuition and provided him with books, food, clothing, and shelter. Graduation day coincided with their divorce. Mr. T argued that since his wife had always worked and he hadn't contributed to her support, he shouldn't be required to pay alimony. However, the court po nted out that while he, by his wife's efforts, had become a professional man, she had remained a secretary. She sacrificed for him in the past and now it was his turn to square things.

A nineteen-year-old Ohio boy married his teen-age sweetheart. Wanting the best for his little girl, the bride's father provided tuition for the boy's education and supplemented his daughter's salary so that the couple could live comfortably while his son-in-law completed school. The lad went through undergraduate studies, medical school, and his internship. Just as he was completing his residency, the marriage lost its luster. The husband claimed that the judge should consider only his meager salary as a resident physician in fixing alimony. True, he had no cash—but his medical license and his future expectations were healthy assets that the court took into account in fixing alimony.

So, in decreeing alimony, the court looks at the husband's "available resources," which may include his earnings, his capacity to earn, stocks and bonds, business interests, property, and so forth. Knowing this and fearful that he may have to support his wife commensurate with his ability, many a chivalrous man will sneak his property into the name of his best friend, deed his real estate to his dad, or make gifts of his bank accounts to his brother. It's his brilliant way of making his available resources unavailable and, of course, as in all such clever schemes, it doesn't work. Parties in divorce suits may be ordered to produce documents showing their income and expenses. So, for example, if our hero's income tax return for the year before the divorce showed interest received on savings accounts and those accounts have magically disappeared, he's got some explaining to do. And if the husband's money is in a bank account, the wife's lawyer can add the bank as another defendant in the divorce suit and ask the judge to issue an injunction against the bank's paying out any of the money until the suit is ended. Likewise, the wife's lawyer can try for an injunction against a profit-sharing fund or family corporation, or the brother-in-law who suddenly acquired title to the husband and wife's house, freezing the assets until the ownership is straightened out.

But figuring out what the husband is worth is only step

one in determining the amount of alimony. Step two is the income and resources of the wife. Here, too, the judge may consider not only the earnings of the woman, but her capacity to earn. If a career woman marries, retires to suburbia, and finds herself in divorce court one year later, she may receive only a moderate allowance payable long enough to support her until she is back into the job market again. It is only in the rare, but enviable, case that alimony will be enough to support a young woman after a brief marriage, clear through old age.

The judge (and the lawyers) will also figure in the age of the parties, their health, and their social standing and status in the community. It is not necessary to be in *Who's Who*, or have "come out" at a debutante cotillion to have social standing and status in the community. After many years of marriage, husband and wife achieve a certain standard of living. It may be a modest standard—that is, they live in a small apartment, they don't take European vacations, she doesn't own furs, and he drives a used car—but their standard is well above that of the people who buy groceries with food stamps, rely on free clinics for medical services, and can't send their children to camp.

Once a couple has established a standard of living, whatever it is, a divorce should not alter it substantially. Suddenly, the wife should not find herself living in a slum project and collecting welfare. As far as practical, she should be able to continue to live after the marriage as she lived before. Alimony allowed Mrs. M to continue with the standard of living established during her marriage—with a strange result. Mr. and Mrs. M lived on the fourth floor of a New York tenement. In the summertime, open windows brought cooking smells, soot, and mosquitoes into their flat. The winter was marked by snow piled on the inside windowsills and frozen water pipes. Only once in the many years of their marriage had Mr. M taken his wife on vacation and then it was to Atlantic

City where the salt water taffy dislodged her bridge and she ate nothing but breakfast cereal for five days. Except for that excursion, Mr. M spent every day in his shoe store. The windows behind the metal grates were never washed, the same red sandals were displayed right through Christmas, and galoshes were hung on clips on a rack brought out whenever it rained. Mrs. M went from store to store seeking out the best prices on lettuce and ground chuck. It was not until their divorce case that Mrs. M learned of the bank accounts filled with money, the safe deposit box filled with money, and the galoshes filled with money. But she couldn't touch it. Mr. and Mrs. M had established a "social standing and status in the community." Mrs. M received only as much alimony as would allow her to live on as she had.

While the lawyers and the judges may not admit it, there are other unofficial facts that go into the determination of alimony. There's the little matter of how much "guilt" may have an emotional impact on the court. If the judge hears a tale of woe told by a bruised and battered woman, mightn't he award her a bit more alimony than he would if she complained only of mental cruelty? If the man of the family has a certain renown or standing in the community, is he likely to agree to pay higher alimony rather than expose his personal and professional reputation to charges of adultery? Will the husband who wants a quicky divorce so he can have a quicky remarriage pay just a bit more so he doesn't have to wait for the judge to hear a contested lawsuit? Will a woman accept less to protect her children from a bad press? A touch of blackmail, a shade of extortion, a slight nuance of highway robbery—although unarticulated—often do creep into the negotiations over alimony.

Add to these factors the relative skills of your lawyer and his, and, sad to say, the actual dollar amount of alimony is still likely to be disappointing. Add together child support and alimony and they rarely equal more than 35 percent of a man's income. So he lives on 65 percent and you and your children subsist on what's left. If there are five children, figure about 50 percent of his income so that alimony and child support leaves him still with half of his salary and the other half is for the six of you. Don't be surprised to find that you are brushing up on your shorthand and typing and looking for a part-time job.

Little if anything said in this chapter (or anywhere else in this book) will differ for people who live in Texas, Arizona, New Mexico, or any of the other "community property" states. The principle of community property does not come from the English common law, which is the basis for most law, but, rather, from states with a Spanish civil law background.

Pick a state that has historic Catholic missions, tile-roofed buildings, cities named after saints, and odds are you've chosen a community property state. Community property declares that the property acquired by either spouse during the marriage belongs to the "marital community"—not to either spouse. When this "marital community" breaks up, the community property gets divided up.

Contrary to its terrific publicity, the dividing up of community property is rarely any different than the dividing up of property of spouses divorced in common-law states. Judges in community property states still have discretion over the division (and it's not always 50-50). In no-fault, community property states, the judge must divide the community equally, *unless* there is a property settlement agreement that provides otherwise. Then there's the involved legal question of which property is part of the community—his inheritance? her birthday gifts? Alimony, that viable and venerable institution, is available in community property states to provide for the support and maintenance of the wife just as in common-law states.

How and When Alimony is Paid

Purists may favor alimony paid in a fixed amount by check

every week. And there's nothing wrong with this approach.

However, instead of the regular weekly installments, alimony also may be paid in one lump sum. Lawyers call it "alimony in gross," and the first consideration here is how gross the lump sum will be. If your ex has boats and cars and property and all of those goodies, and can pay one fat figure, you can accept one lump sum payment of alimony and forget him. Lump sum alimony also has some income tax advantages for you.* It means, too, that once the check is cashed you need never bother with him (or he with you) again—unless, of course, there are children and then he's around to visit and to pay child support.

Lump sum alimony is a profitable idea if you're young and pretty and may remarry soon, or even if you're not so young and not so pretty, but have a boyfriend and will definitely remarry soon. Remember, by statute or by custom, alimony almost always ends when the woman remarries. Her former husband's obligation to see to her support stops when the next husband takes over. Now if you've divorced husband number one and he is paying $50.00 a week in alimony, and you remarry after five weeks, you've got $250. If husband number one agrees to pay you a lump sum of $5,000 and that finishes his obligation—and five weeks later you remarry —well, you're $4,750 ahead. You can buy yourself a nice trousseau, some towels embroidered with your new initials, and still have some cash left. If your first husband is loaded, he may be paying installment alimony of $500 a week, and that in itself may keep you from remarriage. It's true love that will compel a woman to give up her healthy alimony check to marry again to a man whose earnings are just average. So, lump sum alimony may even be an incentive to remarriage. It may also give you the incentive you need to finish your education or invest in a business and launch your career.

---

* Read up on this in chapter twenty-three.

In other words, a lump sum settlement may give you the means to support yourself for the rest of your life without having to accept the allowance your ex sneeringly doles out. Alimony in gross, though, does have its drawbacks. It ends so soon; one payment and never again. Even if he turns around and discovers oil—you'll never get another dime. And if you take every dime and invest in an oil well that delivers nothing but dust, you've had it.

Or why not combine alimony in gross with alimony in installments? This can be a lump sum paid out over several years. For example, you agree to a total sum of $10,000 paid at a rate of $84.00 a month for ten years.* Or perhaps you receive half of the savings accounts now and a small allowance every month later.

Now if the standard weekly allowance until death or remarriage still appeals to you, how about considering a "sliding scale" to determine the amount? For example, if a young doctor is earning $4,000 this year as an intern, $20.00 a week may be all you can receive in alimony. If next year he establishes a practice and earns $10,000 a year, you are still stuck at $20.00 a week until you decide to go back to the divorce court for a post-decree proceeding** to try for more. But, if you've agreed to a sliding scale, this trip to court may be unnecessary. This is how it works. The wife agrees to alimony equal to 20 percent of her husband's income (after he's allowed certain deductions). The first year our young doctor may pay her $10.00 a week, but he must produce his income tax return at the end of the year. If his income tax return shows his yearly income increased to $10,000, her alimony goes to 20 percent of that figure—$2,000 a year, or about $38.00 a week. If next year he earns $15,000, her alimony is 20 percent of that amount, or $3,000 a year, paid

---

* This system also has some income tax effects to consider; see chapter twenty-three.

** The post-decree proceedings are explained in chapter twenty-six.

weekly at about $57.00 a week, and so on. But remember, sliding scales slide down as well as up, so it's nice to try for a "floor"—that is, a statement that no matter how poorly he does, he'll always have to pay $＿＿ (a minimum amount) anyway.

Alimony may be paid in any number of styles and sometimes the fancier, more innovative plans work out better. If the clever accounting schemes appeal to you (and add up to more attractive figures), the plan should be arranged by the lawyers in their negotiations and then taken to the judge for his approval. If the judge has to order alimony from scratch (the lawyers having reached no agreement at all), the judge will be unlikely to go into the mental gymnastics you desire. He's far more likely to lay out a flat figure, payable weekly.

If you've been wondering how the housewife eats and pays the rent while the lawyers haggle and justice snailspaces forward, wonder no more. After the suit is started and immediately after the husband is served with the complaint and summons, the wife's lawyer may move the court for an order granting temporary alimony. The husband will appear with his lawyer and the judge will hold a sort of "mini-trial" to find out what the husband's take-home pay is, whether the wife has an income, and what she needs to get along while the case is pending in court. The judge then enters a temporary order, effective only until the final decree is rendered, setting forth a temporary alimony allowance that is usually a flat figure paid weekly or every payday.

Alimony and Woman's Liberation

Ladies, women, Ms. of the world, and men should unite one and all with woman's lib. As I understand it, the liberation movement doesn't say women must work outside the home and abandon their children to a child care center. It says they may. They may take equal jobs. They may earn equal pay. They may stay home with the kids. They may support their husbands while the men stay home with the kids. The liberation movement is trying to make the choices available. Alimony has become essential in the traditional setting when wife becomes mother and full-time homemaker and where husband brings home the salary. Alimony is a factor, too, where the husband can earn $50,000 a year and the wife is trained for, available for, and employed at a whopping buck and a half an hour. Even now, alimony may provide the initial financial assist to put an erstwhile housewife through professional or trade school.

If both husband and wife are working and earning equivalent incomes, alimony is rarely granted. Come the revolution, and alimony will be paid to the spouse who is not an outside wage earner by the spouse who is—be that wage earner male or female. In many states now, women can be required to pay alimony to men under those circumstances—it's not the law, but the circumstance that's rare.

It seems to me that it's the men who have the greatest chance of "liberation" should woman's lib become a reality. But will someone please explain why it is that the men who howl the loudest over having to pay alimony are the first to declare that "a woman's place is in the home"?

23

Income Tax

Isn't it enough that your husband left you and took the color TV with him, and your daughter is crying because you made daddy go away, and your lawyer won't tell you what's going on, but your parents insist on telling you where you've failed? Does Uncle Sam have to butt in, too?

Joint Tax Returns

For years your husband has been shoving under your nose a joint income tax return he labored over and for years you've signed it without even reading it. Now you're a single woman, or about to be, and that makes you a full-fledged, independent, and tax-paying citizen.

In order to file a joint income tax return, the government says the joint taxpayers must be married. So, once divorced, the taxpayer is a single person and must file a separate income tax return. When the husband is working and the wife is not, or when the husband's salary is much bigger than the wife's, a joint income tax return can save tax money. No matter how bitter the court proceedings, how hot the contest, or how hard the husband tries to conceal his assets from a wife who is trying for alimony and a healthy child support allowance, if they are legally still husband and wife at income tax time, you can bet our male will prepare a joint tax return. There is almost something un-American about paying more income tax than you have to. Our typical male believes that he can still place that joint tax return into his wife's hand, slide a pen between her fingers, and that she'll sign that return this year as she has done every other year before—STOP! If he's been concealing assets from you and your lawyer, that joint tax return just may lead you to the sock in which the money is hidden. Read that return, photocopy it, ask questions about it, send it in to your lawyer, but, for heaven's sake, don't just sign it and return it.

Alimony

Now if you are about to be the gay divorcee and the questions of alimony and child support are still being hammered out, the income tax consequences should be considered. There are some special income tax laws for divorced people, and it's worth the trouble to figure out what they mean to you in dollars and cents.

It may surprise or shock you to learn that alimony is "income" to the wife for income tax purposes. That sweet pension for good and faithful housekeeping services is subject to income tax, and the lady receiving it had better declare her alimony and pay the tax on it. Here's another galling fact. The man who pays out alimony can deduct it from his income tax return.

Let's assume that after fifteen of the best years of your life, you're divorced. He pays $50.00 a week in alimony, which you naturally have to supplement in order to eat. Because your professional training is excellent and because you haven't been in the job market for all those years of diaper changing, you find a stimulating career as a file clerk, working five hours a day while the kids are in school. Your salary is a rousing $60.00 a week. Add up both the salary and the alimony—you pay income tax on both. Meanwhile, our hero is paying out $50.00 a week and deducting it on his income tax return. So, before you sign any property settlement agreement, figure out what you will have left to live on *after* taxes.

If you've chosen alimony in gross, that is, one lump sum and not another dime, you don't pay income tax on the "lump" and your ex doesn't get a deduction either. If the lump sum is payable in installments, there's still no "income" to the wife and no deduction to the husband, unless the installments stretch out over ten years. Then the installments are considered to be "income" to the wife and deductions to the husband.

If Jet-Setter Baby Jane Hi-There divorces her super-rich spouse, and they agree on lump sum alimony of a cool million, Baby pays no income tax and Mr. Hi-There gets no deduction. But, if Baby takes her million in installments of $50,000 a year for twenty years, then she's stuck with a fat income tax. Every year like clockwork Uncle Sam will be around collecting his share of her alimony, while her spouse is saving tax by deducting that $50,000 from his income. If, instead of paying Baby Jane in cash, Hi-There delivers shares of stock having a value of $50,000 a year or $1,000,000, just once, then the government may say that Hi-There is transferring his shares just as if he had sold them on the market, and he might be stuck with a tax on the transfer of a capital asset.

For those fortunate people who worry about such things as long-term capital gains, investment credits, and tax brackets, the decision of whether to pay or receive alimony in installments or in gross may have to be made with an

accountant at their elbow. Emotions aside, vengeance forgotten, the amount and method of paying and receiving
alimony may be a cold, hard decision dictated by the Internal
Revenue Code.

Child Support

Fathers have to support their children. They have to provide
the cash for food, shelter, clothing, and guitar lessons whether
they are married or divorced. Since they are stuck with this
duty anyway, dad gets no deduction for the child support he
pays and mom pays no income tax on the child support she
receives. This is not the end of the income tax story, but
only the beginning.

Unless the government scrambles the tax return form again
in its never-ending quest to render the taxpayer crazy as well
as broke, you will find at the upper right-hand corner of the
first page of the 1040 return, a convenient box for the adding
up of personal exemptions. If you're under sixty-five and have
decent vision, you'll mark down one exemption for yourself.
Since you no longer have a spouse, you have no exemption
there. Now move down to the next line—the names of your
dependent children. Are the children who live with you,
eat what you cook, wear what you iron, and keep you up all
night when they're sick, "dependent"? Maybe. Your dependent, according to the IRS, is someone who gets more than
one-half of his *financial* support from you. The divorced
parent who provides more than one-half of the cash to pay
for whatever is needed to provide for his child is entitled to
the $750 exemption. He or she can claim that child as a
dependent in figuring out how much tax to pay by using the
tables at the back of the return. Figuring out the father's share
of support for the child is easy. If his child support payment
is $10.00 a week, he has paid $520 a year toward the child's
support.

The tough question is whether you've contributed more

than half of the cash needed to support your offspring. This may take a full-time bookkeeping system and higher mathematics. First, figure the child's share of the rent, the food budget, utilities, the cost of his clothing, his medical bills, the dentist, school tuition, the school bus, outings, birthday parties, ballet lessons, and so on. Add up the outlay and if the child has "spent" more than $1,040, that is, more than twice what his dad supplied in child support, the child is *your* dependent and your precious little exemption.

Needless to say, the issue of who gets to claim junior as a dependent haunts the Internal Revenue Service. Fathers who never raised a finger to win custody of their children, and who howl and carry on like martyrs when they must contribute to their children's support, always, always claim the children as *their* dependents when tax time comes around. In comes mama with a tax return claiming that same child as her exemption and a schedule listing every Popsicle, every shoelace, every bottle of calamine lotion she purchased during the year. Faced with those circumstances, the IRS further confused the issue by deciding that:

(1) General rule.—If—
    (A) a child (as defined in section 151(e) (3)) receives over half of his support during the calendar year from his parents who are divorced or legally separated under a decree of divorce or separate maintenance, or who are separated under a written separation agreement, and
    (B) such child is in the custody of one or both of his parents for more than one-half of the calendar year,
such child shall be treated, for purposes of subsection (a), as receiving over half of his support during the calendar year from the parent having custody for a greater portion of the calendar year unless he is treated, under the provisions of paragraph (2), as having received over half of his support for such year from the other parent (referred to in this subsection as the parent not having custody).

(2) Special rule.—The child of parents described in paragraph (1) shall be treated as having received over half of his support during the calendar year from the parent not having custody if—

(A) (i) the decree of divorce or of separate maintenance, or a written agreement between the parents applicable to the taxable year beginning in such calendar year, provides that the parent not having custody shall be entitled to any deduction allowable under section 151 for such child; and

(ii) such parent not having custody provides at least $600 for the support of such child during the calendar year, or

(B) (i) the parent not having custody provides $1,200 or more for the support of such child (or if there is more than one such child, $1,200 or more for all of such children) for the calendar year, and

(ii) the parent having custody of such child does not clearly establish that he provided more for the support of such child during the calendar year than the parent not having custody.

For the purposes of this paragraph, amounts expended for the support of a child or children shall be treated as received from the parent not having custody to the extent that such parent provided amounts for such support.

(3) Itemized statement required.—If a taxpayer claims that paragraph (2) (B) applies with respect to a child for a calendar year and the other parent claims that paragraph (2) (B) (i) is not satisfied or claims to have provided more for the support of such child during such calendar year than the taxpayer, each parent shall be entitled to receive, under regulations to be prescribed by the Secretary or his delegate, an itemized statement of the expenditures upon which the other parent's claim of support is based.

(4) Exception for multiple-support agreement.—The provisions of this subsection shall not apply in any case where over half of the support of the child is treated as having been received from a taxpayer under the provisions of subsection (c).

(5) Regulations.—The Secretary or his delegate shall prescribe

such regulations as may be necessary to carry out the purposes of this subsection.

The point of this crystal-clear provision is that the Internal Revenue Service fervently prays that when husband and wife enter into a property settlement agreement, they will agree, in writing, that one or the other of them will take all, some, or one of the children as dependents on their tax returns forever into the future. Since the IRS seems to delight in auditing the returns of ordinary folks, such an agreement as to who takes whom on whose return may save you a few trips to the government office and undoubtedly will free you from saving receipts from the Good Humor man.

And, as long as we're being so agreeable, consider whether the circumstances warrant your entering into a "multiple support agreement." If their dad is providing 35 percent of the kid's support and you are providing 25 percent of their support, and your dad is contributing and providing 40 percent of his grandchildren's support, the thing to do is to enter into an agreement that allows one of the three of you to take the kids as deductions. Multiple support agreements (another snappy phrase thought up by the IRS) are handy when more than two people are sharing in the support obligations. Getting together may mean that the person with the most income and the highest tax gets the deduction. This is perfectly legal and can save some tax money *if* you all can agree on who's entitled to the saving.

Deducting Legal Fees

Fees paid to lawyers who perform personal services are not deductible on their client's income tax return. Since divorce is clearly "personal" and, I trust, not part of the spouse's "trade or business," the fee paid is gone forever without even a deduction for income tax. But all is not lost.

The Internal Revenue Code says that it's permissible to

deduct for professional services for income tax advice. Lawyers who respect their clients (and who hold out the hope of billing and collecting for their services) keep records of what they do to earn their fees. When the lady hangs up the phone after asking her lawyer whether she has to pay income tax on her alimony, the lawyer writes down on his time record something like "Teleconf. with Mrs. R re taxability of alimony—¼ hr." When the lawyer sends his bill, he should itemize what portion is payable for the usual divorce work and what part is for tax consultation. If he forgets, remind him. The part of the lawyer's fee that he allocated to income tax advice is a deduction on your tax return. Small savings like this make that fee a mite easier to pay.

24

The Property Settlement Agreement

REMEMBER the night, the night you said, "I hate you"? Remember the night he came in at 2:00 A.M. and forgot to mention he wasn't coming home for dinner? Do you recall the evening he said he was working late, and you called the office and the phone rang and rang? What about the battle over his mother, your father, borrowing against the mortgage on the house, your friends, his poker night? All of the screaming, the tantrums, and the door slamming may only be minor skirmishes compared to the Armageddon of dividing up the household furniture, the camera and projector, and the car. The "friendliest" divorce can reduce itself to a hair-pulling and hair-splitting tug-of-war when it's time to divide up the TV.

What Is a Property Settlement Agreement?
The property settlement agreement is first and foremost a "settlement." It is the written contract that says "we've

decided not to contest the division of property in court."
It is not an agreement that the plaintiff will actually win
the divorce decree. That is up to the judge, and evidence
must be presented showing that the plaintiff in the case has
grounds and is entitled to be divorced. The property settlement agreement settles only the question of who gets what
property *if* the marriage is dissolved.

In the absence of a "settlement," the divorce court judge
will decide who gets what. Divorce courts throughout the
country are busy places these days. Divorce court judges are
harried, worried men who pass one-half of their careers
being bored hearing routine default divorce cases and the
other half working up ulcers and heart attacks, hearing
evidence, and deciding questions ranging from who gets
grandma's stemware to who gets custody of the children.
They rightly expect the lawyers to work out settlements that
dispose of the family jewels, divide up the bank accounts,
and decide who lives in the house and who pays the mortgage
on it. No judge, no matter how wise, how patient, or how
compassionate, is going to lose sleep over whether you can
keep the movie camera and the films of your offspring's first
birthday party. These matters are best decided in a lawyer's
office, not in the courthouse.

Then there's the fact that no matter how right you are
and how sure you are that you're right, you may go into
court and find that the judge doesn't agree with you on
anything. He's having a bad day, or he sees the other side of
the story (which is, after all, his job), or he doesn't like you,
or your lawyer antagonized him in a case he tried a month
ago. The truth is that judges are human. If a judge rules
against you on the question of who gets the car, there are
only three alternatives. The first alternative is that you
laughingly turn over the car keys, unlock the garage door,
and watch your ex smugly drive off. The second alternative
is that you refuse to surrender the car and are sent to jail for

contempt of court (and in jail, there's precious little opportunity for a Sunday drive). The third alternative is that you
appeal the judge's decision, and even if the auto is a classic
Rolls, the legal fees and appeals costs may exceed its value—
and then you still can lose.

Settlement of the property rights is not only the simplest,
cheapest, and least emotional approach, it may be the only
way to assure that when the dust settles, you are not abandoned
and wearing your one remaining bath towel. The property
settlement agreement gives you the "bird in the hand."

When Is the Agreement Entered Into?

As soon as the complaint for divorce is on file and the case
is started, the lawyers will launch into the bargaining,
mongering, and negotiating over the terms of the property
settlement agreement. Needless to say, the more property
involved, the more energy, concentration, and $50-an-hour
time will be spent.

The property settlement agreement is drafted and signed
after the divorce suit is filed and *before* the decree is entered.
Sometimes a property settlement of sorts is prepared before
the parties marry. This is known as an "Antenuptial Agreement." Others are prepared after the wedding, but before
the divorce. These are "Postnuptial Agreements." Both are
most commonly used when the bride and groom are older,
have estates from their deceased first spouses, and each have
their own children. These newlyweds want their own
children to inherit from their own personal estates, and
they don't want their new spouses to share in an inheritance
that comes from property each earned or each received from
his deceased first spouse.

Antenuptial and postnuptial agreements are quite acceptable—but they are *not* property settlement agreements. The
property settlement agreement contemplates that a divorce
will be granted and provides for who gets what should the

judge dissolve the bonds of matrimony. Antenuptial and postnuptial agreements decide who gets what on death, but they do not and cannot contemplate or plan for divorce. That would be against public policy.

Once again, remember, there are three parties to every marriage: the husband, the wife, and the state. The state blindly, and romantically, says that all marriages work 'til death do us part. It is against the policy of the state for a married couple to sit down and figure out what will happen to the house or how much alimony the wife will get if they divorce. Thus, any agreement that tries to fix the rights and obligations of a couple in the event of divorce is void. Any agreement, that is, except a property settlement agreement that is entered into to settle property rights *after* a divorce suit has already been filed. If the divorce suit is filed and then withdrawn, or if the judge denies the divorce, the property settlement agreement becomes a postnuptial agreement fixing rights in the event of divorce and it is *void* and absolutely meaningless.

While the property settlement agreement theoretically can be entered into *after* the decree for divorce, it shouldn't be. Once the judge decrees the divorce, he says "the marriage is over, you're both single people, and I have nothing more to say." The divorce court no longer has jurisdiction, the right to speak about the marriage or the marital property. The woman who has no property settlement and no court decree dividing property has little or no chance to anything once the decree is entered. She has no law to help her, no judge to hear her, and no bargaining power. She has only to wait around for the crust of bread her former husband may toss her way.

Prerequisites to a Valid Agreement

In order for the agreement to be valid, the division of property must take place after the husband and wife have decided to go their separate ways and after they have filed for divorce as proof of their decision.

A property settlement agreement will be invalid unless the parties have entered into it freely and not as the result of threats. Mrs. R signed a property settlement agreement giving up all of her rights to community property, any claim to child custody or visitation, all alimony, and every stick of furniture. Mrs. R had fallen right into an adulterous affair, and her husband threatened to expose the whole sordid mess if she didn't sign. (That case was heard in the Supreme Court of Washington at the turn of the century when such disclosures mattered.) But the judge heard evidence that Mr. R beat and kicked his wife regularly and slapped her when she didn't get up to milk the cows the day after the birth of their child. The judge, a true romantic, declared that Mr. R drove his wife into the arms of a sympathetic man and while the law wouldn't excuse her, it would understand. The property settlement agreement was set aside.

In order for it to be a fair agreement, both parties must know exactly what property each has. The job, then, is finding out exactly what the husband is worth and what the wife has salted away. A property settlement agreement may be set aside, held for naught, and used to wrap the garbage unless there is full disclosure of each party's assets. The poor, poor husband who discloses as his sole possessions a pair of bent cuff links, a seashell, a lucky half-dollar, and some string he's saved, and who signs a property settlement dividing those up, gets divorced, and then drives off in a shiny Mercedes is just begging to have the agreement set aside. When entering into the property settlement agreement, the spouses have the choice of full disclosure or of spending the rest of their lives living in abject poverty so the other doesn't find out what was concealed.

Incorporating the Agreement into the Decree

Once the property settlement agreement is freely signed after full disclosure, it becomes a contract, binding from the day the divorce decree is entered. If one party to a contract fails to perform, he may be sued for breach of contract. This is the usual way to enforce a contract when one side decides he doesn't want to carry out his part of the agreement. So the parties go back to court, in a long, drawn-out, and expensive suit.

A shortcut also is available to divorcing parties who enter into property settlements. At the time of the trial of the divorce case, the lawyer may submit the property settlement agreement to the judge. If the judge is satisfied that the agreement is fair under the circumstances of the case (and he almost always is satisfied with the end-product of two lawyers' best efforts to divide up the family wealth and satisfy each of their clients), the judge may incorporate the property settlement agreement into his decree for divorce. This is not just a legal nicety that allows your property settlement to be attached to the decree in a fancy blue cover. When the judge incorporates the property settlement agreement into his decree, he makes the terms of the settlement a court order. The spouse who fails to perform according to the agreement is not only in breach of contract, he's in contempt of court. When he "forgets" to send the alimony provided in paragraph ten of the agreement, he is "forgetting" to follow the judge's order and you can run right back to court for a posthaste order either that he pay up or cool off in jail.

An agreement that is not a part of the decree, but is simply a contract between spouses, may not be subject to modification later. If the wife agrees to alimony of $50.00 a month for life, it matters little that the husband one day may actually make the fortune she thought he would when she married him. If though, the property settlement agreement is part and parcel of the divorce decree, it, like the decree, is subject to the continuing jurisdiction of the divorce court. That is, the judge may decide that a man who has made the cover of *Time* may well be able to kick in a bit more than he agreed to pay when he was working his way up to the Nobel Prize.

Contents of the Agreement

The question is: What rights does the agreement settle? The answer is this: The agreement can and should settle everything so that there are no leftover unaccounted-for goodies. All the loose ends ranging from child custody, support, and visitation, right down to the fishing tackle you'd love to have him remove from the basement can be tied up in a well-prepared property settlement agreement. Whatever rights the law creates in property owned by married people, a property settlement agreement can alter, amend, or undo. By whatever means the husband and wife hold legal title to their property, the property settlement agreement can provide the method for changing the title. But before altering, amending, or undoing property rights, the spouse should know what those rights are.

Most of the things you own are yours because you've paid for them and are holding on to them. When you buy a dress, you pay for it, carry it home, and hang it in your closet. It's yours. Legally, it becomes yours when you hand over the money and receive the parcel; title to the dress then passes from the store to you. But possession isn't enough to prove ownership of many kinds of property. For example, the tenant living in apartment 3472A of a giant apartment building probably owns neither the apartment nor the building—even though he "possesses" his flat. Title to the real estate is written into a deed and recorded each time the property is sold. Holding on to a savings account passbook doesn't mean "ownership" of the account. Title to the account is determined by the names on the bank's signature cards. Nor are stock certificates owned by the person who stashes them in a secret hiding place. The corporation that issues the stock lists its shareholders on the corporate records.

When people go to the trouble of signing deeds, recording certificates, opening bank accounts, and so forth, they usually are required to decide how "title," the evidence of ownership, will be held. One way of holding title is called "joint tenancy." This is perhaps the most common way that married people hold title to their property. The deed to the bi-level may pass title "to Joe Suburbia and Jane Suburbia, his wife, as joint tenants." Translating that from common-law language, that means that both Joe and Jane own the house together and if one of them dies, the other automatically will own the whole house. Now, if the house is owned in joint tenancy, but the marriage is breaking up, the property settlement agreement can give Jane the exclusive right to live in the house with Joe having to find his own apartment in town, but title can stay in joint tenancy. That means that if Jane dies first, Joe owns the bi-level and can live in it or sell it as he pleases. If Joe dies first, Jane owns it exclusively. Or, the property settlement agreement may say that Joe will deed the house to Jane so that he will not only give possession to Jane, but title will be changed, too, and Jane will own the house and do with it exactly as she pleases—sell it, live in it, or will it to her boyfriend when she dies.

Anybody can own property in joint tenancy; husband and wife, business partners, mother and daughter, ten people, or two people. Divorce doesn't necessarily mean that title to the house can't stay as it was, in joint tenancy. If possible though, it's best not only that you win exclusive possession, but that he deed the title to you. That way, you can turn around and sell it for a quick profit without having to get his signature on the deed (for which he'll undoubtedly want a cut of the profit), or you m y live in the house and add a paneled den without enhancing *his* property, and you can will it to whomever you wish.

When married people open bank accounts, they often put their savings into joint tenancy. The bank's records show that account number 22458 is owned by Sam Spendthrift and Sally Spendthrift, husband and wife, in joint tenancy. If Sam dies before Sally, she is the automatic owner of the account, and vice versa. During their lives, either joint tenant can deposit money in the account and either can withdraw it. The joint tenancy bank account is the basis and inspiration for the Grand Prix of divorce. This is the race, more time-honored than Ascot, where the divorcing husband and the divorcing wife run from their lawyers' offices to the bank and the first one there with the passbook claims neither a blanket of roses nor a gold cup, but the balance in the joint account.

If you enter this race and win, you get the cash and while the divorce suit goes on, there's some money to spend on the niceties of life, like food and shelter. On the other hand, the trumpets that sound the entry into this race may be ringing the death knell to a reconcilable marriage. A husband who still has tender feelings for his wife and feels guilt over his misbehavior will develop a thoroughgoing hatred for the woman who cleaned out the savings account. Furthermore, all of his guilt will be cleansed and his acts appear justified when he writes a check that bounces because his wife withdrew the balance in their joint checking account. Then, too, a judge who would sympathetically award a divorcing wife the temporary alimony, child support, and attorney's fees she needs while the suit is pending, may order her to pay her own way with the money she's won in the race to the bank.

Some states still recognize "tenancy by the entirety," which, while out of vogue and abandoned almost everywhere, is a method of holding title between husband and wife. The tenants by the entireties each own property with the right to the whole title automatically to the spouse who survives his mate. In other words, tenancy by the entirety is exactly the same as joint tenancy, except that it's allowed between husband and wife only. A divorce then automatically affects title held by the entireties and turns it into "tenancy in common."

"Tenancy in common" describes title held by two or more people as partners. Each owner may deed his share to someone else, and each may pass his share by will on his death to whomever he wishes. If a divorced wife then wills her share of the tenancy in common title of the marital home to her lover, he and her former husband will find themselves as real estate partners.

Whether title is joint, by the entireties, or in common, a divorcing spouse will generally have difficulty selling without the other's approval and won't have freedom to will the property (even if it's in tenancy in common, unless she doesn't mind putting her beneficiary and her ex in partnership). The property settlement agreement will settle most matters if the title is divided up once and for all—she gets the house, he gets the stocks and bonds, and so forth. If the partnership didn't work out while the couple was married, it probably will be all the more difficult afterwards.

For many married couples the house is the one valuable item of property. The savings account is nonexistent, the checking account balance is precarious, and the only stocks and bonds are a few Series E's bought out of a 25¢-a-week schoolroom collection during World War II. If there are no little children living in the house with mom, one can hardly blame a man for wanting some cash out of the house he's been paying for. It's always possible to sell the house and divide up the proceeds. And if man and wife can't agree who is to take possession of the house, or what to do with the title, a judge has the power to order that the place be put on the market and sold to the highest bidder, and that the parties split the profits (and the split is not always 50-50).

Community property may be negotiated over and divided up in a property settlement agreement just like any other property. As stated earlier, most of U.S. law is based on the English common-law tradition, but a few states (Texas and California, for example), still have laws established during the days of the conquistadores. Community property simply means that all the property acquired by either spouse during the marriage is considered to be owned by both parties of the marriage. When the marriage is being dissolved by divorce, the job then is to decide who owns what property separately and how the community property gets divided.

There are some rules for deciding what is owned by the "marital community" and what isn't. For example, stock owned by one spouse before marriage is separate property, but dividends earned on it during marriage are community. Real estate may be separate property, but rents received on it during marriage are part of the community, and so forth. The problems of deciding who can claim ownership of what property could be difficult if it weren't that in both community property and common-law states every asset owned by the wife and every asset of the husband is fair ground for property division in divorce. It rarely matters whether the gypsy girl painting above the couch is his, hers, or the community's; only one spouse will get it.

A Sample Property Settlement Agreement

No combination of words is magic, no two lawyers will draft an identical property settlement agreement (unless one of them is copying), agreements vary with state laws, and no lawyer is smarter than your lawyer, whoever he is. Having said all of that, what follows is a sample of what a property settlement agreement might look like.

The introductory paragraph tells who the parties to the

agreement are, when they signed the agreement, and where they reside.

PROPERTY SETTLEMENT AGREEMENT

THIS AGREEMENT is made and entered into this _____ day of _____, 19___, by and between _____, herein referred to as "wife," and _____, herein referred to as "husband:" both parties of the City of _____, County of _____ , and State of _____ .

The next section of the agreement has the "Whereas" sections that explain how the parties got to their present situation.

WHEREAS, the said parties are now husband and wife having been married on_____ at _____; and

WHEREAS, irreconcilable differences have arisen between the parties, who are now and have been estranged from each other and are not living together as husband and wife;

The next "Whereas" paragraphs show that the agreement is a "property settlement" agreement written *after* the suit was filed, but *before* the divorce is granted.

WHEREAS, the wife has filed a Complaint for Divorce in the Circuit Court of _____ County _____, known as Case No. _____ and entitled (wife's name), plaintiff v. (husband's name), defendant, and this case is pending and undetermined; and

WHEREAS, the parties hereby consider it to their best interest to settle between themselves now and forever their respective rights of property, dower rights, homestead rights, rights to support, and any and all other rights of property and otherwise growing out of the marriage relationship existing between them and which either of them now has, or may hereafter have or claim to have against the other, and all rights of any kind, nature and description which either of them now has or may hereafter have or claim to have, in and to any property of every kind, nature, and description, real, personal, and mixed, now owned by or which may hereafter be acquired by either of them, EXCEPT as hereinafter set forth with respect to the continuing jurisdiction of the Circuit Court of _____ County, _____, to modify or alter this agreement as to matters not waived herein, should it become a part of the decree of divorce hereinafter referred to;

The two following paragraphs show that each party had a lawyer (or was advised of his right to have a lawyer) and that both the husband and the wife told each other about all of their property.

WHEREAS, the wife is represented by   (her lawyer), and the husband is represented by   (his lawyer)   , and the parties have had the benefit of the advice and counsel of their respective attorneys; and

WHEREAS, each party has made full disclosure to the other of all properties owned by each of them and of the income derived therefrom and from all other sources;

Next follows the fancy legal language that explains that each is giving the other some benefit so that what follows is a fair bargain.

NOW THEREFORE, in consideration of the mutual promises and other good and valuable consideration hereto expressed, the sufficiency of which consideration is hereby acknowledged, the parties hereto agree as follows:

Here goes. The first paragraph may deal with alimony in a weekly amount.

That the husband is presently employed and in receipt of

a salary of $_____ per week, which is "net" after deductions for social security, taxes (both state and federal), and insurance, which is deducted from his paycheck; the wife is presently seeking part-time employment but has been unemployed outside the home during the marriage; based on their respective incomes (and in the case of the wife, her expectation of income from part-time employment should she be able to obtain same), the husband agrees to pay to the wife as and for alimony the sum of $_____ per month; the first payment to be made upon the entry of a Decree of Divorce in the pending suit and subsequent payments to be made on the first day of each succeeding month. This alimony shall end on the remarriage of the wife, death of the wife, or death of the husband.

Or, it may provide for alimony in gross.

That the husband is presently employed and in receipt of a substantial salary of $_____ per week, which is "net" after deductions for social security and taxes (both state and federal); and the wife is presently employed and in receipt of a gross salary of $_____ per week; that based on their respective incomes, the husband agrees to pay to the wife as and for alimony the sum of $_____, the payment of the full amount to be made upon the entry of a Decree of Divorce in the pending suit, and in consideration of said payment, the wife expressly waives alimony and said payment shall be deemed in lieu of alimony.

Or, it may provide for a complete waiver of alimony.

That the husband is presently employed and in receipt of a gross salary of $_____ per year; the wife is presently employed and earns a gross salary of $_____ per year; and based on their respective incomes, the husband and wife each agree to waive alimony.

Alimony can be based on a percentage or be subject to an escalator clause. The possibilities are endless. Here's just one sample of alimony with an escalator based on a percentage of the husband's income reported each year in his income tax return.

That the husband is presently employed and during the calendar year, 1971, was in receipt of the sum of $_____, which figure was "gross," before deductions for social security and taxes, both state and federal, and the wife is presently employed on a part-time basis from her home and when working, receives a salary of $_____ gross per week; that based upon their respective incomes, the husband agrees to pay to the wife as and for alimony a sum equal to _____ percent of his "income" as the term "income" is defined in Paragraph (a) hereinbelow, and as computed herein, payable to the wife on alternating Mondays. This alimony shall end on the remarriage of the wife, death of the wife, or death of the husband.

That the husband shall pay to the wife for the support of the said children a sum equal to _____ percent of his "income" as the term "income" is defined in Paragraph (a) hereinbelow, and as computed herein, payable to the wife on alternating Mondays.

(a) For all purposes herein, the term "income" shall be deemed to mean all items taxable pursuant to the Federal Internal Revenue Code, including wages, salaries, royalties, dividends, interest, commissions, gratuities, and the like, after deductions for payments made by the husband pursuant to the Federal Insurance Contributions Act and after deductions of taxes paid pursuant to Federal and State income tax laws, and after deductions for payments that are deducted from the husband's salary and wages for group insurance and hospitalization insurance.

(b) From the date of the decree of divorce in the hereinabove designated suit for divorce, until April 30, 1973, the husband shall pay to the wife on alternating Mondays, the sum of $_____ as and for alimony, and the sum of $_____ as and for child support.

(c) Commencing April 15, 1973, and each April 15 thereafter, the husband shall present to the wife a true and correct copy of his income tax return for the immediately preceding year covered by said return. The husband's income, as that term is defined in paragraph (a) hereinabove, for the immediately preceding year covered by the said return, shall be divided by twenty-six (26) and _____ percent of that figure shall be alimony payable on alternating Mondays, and _____ percent of that figure shall be child support payable on alternating Mondays; these payments to commence on the next alternating Monday after April 30 of each year.

(d) Notwithstanding anything in paragraph (c) to the contrary, in no event shall payment as and for alimony be less than $____ per month, and in no event shall payment as and for child support be less than $_____ per month so long as both children are eligible for child support. The provisions of this paragraph shall be abrogated in the event the husband is without a source of income through no fault of his own.

Child custody, support, and visitation also can be settled in the agreement. A custody provision may look like this one:

That two children were born to the parties and no other children were born or adopted by them, and that the two children born to the parties are as follows:

(child's name)   (birth date)
(child's name)   (birth date)

That the wife shall have the sole care, custody, education, and control of said children of the parties.

If the wife with custody wants to leave town with the kids, the lawyer will show that the husband is agreeable.

It is expressly understood and agreed by the parties that the wife may leave the jurisdiction with the children and take up residency in _____ .

Visitation should be set forth so that there are few fights later:

The husband shall have the right of reasonable visitation on each Sunday for reasonable daytime hours.

Or, if you can't agree on holiday visitation:

That the husband shall have the right of reasonable visitation on each Sunday or on one other day each week in lieu of Sunday, as may be agreed to from time to time; and the husband agrees that the visitation day shall end and the children will be returned home by 7:00 P.M. The wife agrees that the husband may, in addition to the visitation provided above, have visitation with the children one weekend each month. The husband and wife shall alternate visitation on the following holidays so that the children will spend Christmas 1972 with the wife and Christmas 1973 with the husband, and the children shall spend New Year's Day 1973 with the husband and New Year's Day 1974 with the wife, and so forth. The holidays are as follows: Christmas Day, New Year's Day, Easter, and Thanksgiving. The husband may have visitation each year on Father's Day. The husband shall have visitation for two consecutive weeks each summer.

Child support payments whether weekly, monthly, a fixed figure, or a sliding one should be clearly set forth. A set amount of child support may be decided upon:

The husband shall pay to the wife for the support of said children the sum of $_____ per month, payable on the first day of each month and commencing on the date of the entry of the Decree.

Any number of "escalator" provisions can be figured out for child support. In one situation, the husband's regular salary was small, but his overtime pay was generous and the boss always required his employees to put in plenty of valuable overtime. The wife's lawyer worked out a provision for additional child support every week the husband received overtime pay. This paragraph could also include special provisions for summer camp, religious education, college, special training or support for a handicapped child, and so forth.

That the husband shall pay to the wife for the support of said children, the sum of $_____ per month; the first payment to be made upon the entry of a Decree of Divorce in the pending suit and subsequent payments to be made on the first day of each succeeding month. In addition to the above support sum, the husband shall pay to the wife for the support of said minor children an additional amount equal to one-half (½) of any overtime salary the husband shall receive during any month. This additional amount shall be computed by deducting from the overtime salary any sums deducted for social security, taxes (both state and federal), and insurance customarily deducted from the overtime salary on the paycheck and then dividing that figure in half. This additional payment of support shall be paid on the first day of the month following the entry of the Decree of Divorce in the pending suit and subsequent payments shall be made on the first day of each succeeding month on the basis of any overtime salary the husband shall have received in the month immediately preceding. The husband shall make available to the wife, upon her request, all paycheck "stubs" received by him in each month immediately preceding the month of the wife's request.

Any special income tax considerations can go in this section.

So long as the husband complies with the terms of this Agreement as to child support, he shall be deemed to have provided for more than one-half of their support for income tax purposes; the husband may deduct all payments as and for alimony for income tax purposes, and the wife shall include same as income in her income tax return.

The next section of the agreement can divide up the real estate:

The parties own the property commonly known as   (street address),   holding title as joint tenants with the right of survivorship.

It is agreed that the wife shall have sole possession of said property and that on the day of the entry of the decree herein, the husband shall execute and deliver to the wife a quit claim deed conveying to the wife all right and interest he has or may claim to have in the said property.

The wife agrees that from the date of the delivery of said deed, all obligations for mortgage payments, maintenance, and real estate taxes accruing on said property from the date of the delivery of the deed shall be her sole responsibility.

How about the furniture, car, bank accounts, and so forth?

It is agreed that all household furnishings, furniture, and appliances and personal effects owned by the parties at the marital residence at _____, shall be the sole property of the wife, except that the following shall be the sole property of the husband:

a. The stereophonic record player;
b. The camper trailer;
c. The television set; and
d. The clothing and accessories to the clothing of the husband ·

It is agreed that the savings account at _____ Bank and Trust Company, which has a present balance of approximately $1,600 shall be the sole property of the husband;

It is agreed that the 1970   (automobile)   shall be the property of the husband and the husband shall have sole responsibility for any payments or obligations relating thereto.

The agreement should list the family debts and decide who should pay them. With medical bills as high as they are, it's great if the husband will pay or get insurance to cover at least the major health expenses. This is also the ideal place to state that the husband shall pay all expenses for orthodontists.

It is further agreed that in addition to the payments below and hereinabove provided, the husband shall pay all extraordinary medical, surgical, and dental bills, for the said children.

It is further agreed that in addition to the payments below and hereinabove provided, the husband shall pay all extraordinary medical, surgical, and dental bills of the wife.

The term "extraordinary" shall not include routine checkups, minor ailments, drug supplies incident to the treatment of minor ailments, dental checkups, and the filling of simple cavities and the like.

Many women are surprised to learn that a father may disinherit his children. If he has a will giving every penny to Dora Dimples, the woman who came between you, Dora may be wearing furs while the kids can barely have their sneakers resoled. If he's loaded, the property settlement agreement may include his creating a trust for the children. If he's just an average earner, he can still provide a life insurance policy to protect his children. Consider this:

The husband has heretofore obtained a policy of insurance upon his life, in the course of and as a benefit of his employment, and the husband shall name the two children as irrevocable beneficiaries under said policy and in the event the existing policy is terminated for any reason, the husband shall immediately obtain a policy of insurance upon his life in a face amount of no less than $____ naming the two children as irrevocable beneficiaries. The husband shall not borrow against any such policy or use any such policy as collateral or impair its value in any manner and shall upon the reasonable request of the wife make such policy available for her inspection together with evidence of current payment of premiums.

The paragraph neither your lawyer nor his is likely to overlook, is this one:

> That the husband shall pay to _____, attorney for the wife, upon entry of the decree, the sum of $____, for all legal services to the wife in connection with said suit for divorce, and the husband shall pay all court costs for the wife.

The property settlement agreement should dispose of any possible lawsuits in the future as to who is entitled to what from whom. The final, catch-all paragraph, where each spouse releases the other from any future claims not settled in the agreement, looks like this:

> Except as herein provided, each of the parties hereto does hereby forever waive, release, and quitclaim to the other party all rights of dower, homestead, and all other property rights and claims, which he or she now has or may hereafter have, as husband, wife, widower, widow, or otherwise, by reason of the marital relations now existing between the parties hereto under any present or future law of any State or the United States of America, or of any other country, in or to, or against the property of the other party, or her or his estate, whether now owned or hereafter acquired by such other party. Each of the parties hereto further covenants, and agrees, for himself and herself and his or her heirs, executors, administrators, and assigns, that he or she will never sue the other party or his or her heirs, executors, administrators, or assigns, for the purpose of enforcing any or either of the rights specified in and relinquished under this paragraph.

Finally, the property settlement agreement should be incorporated into the court's Decree for Divorce.

> This Agreement shall be submitted to the court for its approval and if approved, shall be made part of the Decree for Divorce, and shall be of effect and binding only if a decree for

divorce is entered in said pending suit; in the event the said court refuses to grant a decree for divorce in the pending suit, then this Agreement shall be null and void and of no effect whatsoever. It is expressly understood that if the Agreement is approved and made a part of the decree for divorce, it may from time to time be modified in accordance with the continuing jurisdiction of the _____ Court of _____ County and by its order.

Following this, there are lines for signature, for witnesses, for notary seals, everything that makes a legal document look like a legal document.

And that's it. As simple as the United Nations Charter, as informal as the Treaty of Versailles. The property settlement is a truce, the end of hostilities, the silence after Appomattox.

25

In Court

No matter how many television dramas you've watched or how many murder mysteries you've read, the courthouse may seem an alien and forbidding place. The judge, just another man when he's seen on the street in a business suit, is, in the courtroom, a special personage. Clad in the traditional black robe, and sitting at "the bench" he is, indeed, his honor.

The Complaint

The first trip to the courthouse in any divorce case is not the wife's or the husband's. The lawyer makes the first official trip when he "files the Complaint." The complaint (in some states called "the petition," in others "the bill," in others "the libel") is the initial legal document that begins the divorce case.

In the complaint, the lawyer sets forth all of the facts, which, if proven, will entitle the plaintiff (the person com-

180

plaining) to a divorce. The complaint must set forth a *prima facie* case. That is, it must set forth every element the law requires before a divorce may be granted. The complaint will state the names of the parties, the jurisdiction of the court, the particulars as to when and where the parties were married and how many children they have. The complaint then sets forth the grounds for divorce and asks the judge for the appropriate relief: first, a decree of divorce; second, child custody and support; third, alimony, etc.

As the lawyer interviews his client, he makes notes on his long, yellow tablet. From those notes, he drafts a complaint. He then sends the draft on to his client to read and check for accuracy, and so that his client can stop and think again before she starts the suit. In many states, the plaintiff must sign the complaint, swearing that it is truthful, before it is filed. And don't take that oath lightly. A lie on a pleading, a paper filed with the court, is the same as a lie told on the witness stand, and that may result in a prosecution for perjury. While complaints for divorce vary with state law, the initial divorce pleading may look something like this:

STATE OF ——————)
) SS.
COUNTY OF ——————)

IN THE CIRCUIT COURT OF —————— COUNTY
EQUITY DIVISION

MARY SMITH,   )
          Plaintiff,   )
     v.   )   No. 73 D 1234
)
JOHN SMITH,   )
)
          Defendant.)

COMPLAINT FOR DIVORCE

Now comes the plaintiff, MARY SMITH, by her attorney, _____, and complains of defendant, JOHN SMITH, and states and alleges the following:

The court's jurisdiction over the parties and the subject matter of the marriage may read like this:

That the plaintiff is now, and for more than one year continuously and immediately preceding the filing of this Complaint, has been, an actual resident of the City of _____, County of _____, and State of _____.

The complaint then describes when and where the parties were married and if they have children:

That the parties were married on _____, 19 ___, at _____, _____.
That two children were born to the parties and no other children were born or adopted by them, and that the two children born to the parties are as follows:

_____ born _____,
_____ born _____.

The complaint should then state whether the parties are living together or separated, and the complaint can state here that the husband and wife are not having sexual intercourse. Remember the defense of condonation?

That the plaintiff is living in the same house as the defendant, but is occupying a separate room.

OR

That the plaintiff and defendant are, without fault or provocation of the plaintiff, living separate and apart as single persons.

Now, the complaint tells the judge what a faithful, loving wife you always were and what a rat your husband has been. For example:

That at all times the plaintiff has conducted herself as a true, faithful, and affectionate wife.

That the children of the marriage are and have always been residing with their mother, the plaintiff herein.

That the plaintiff is a fit and proper person to have the care, custody, control, and education of said children; that the defendant is unfit because of his (uncontrollable temper) (abusive manner) (indifference) toward said children.

That the defendant, disregarding his marriage vows to the plaintiff, has since their marriage, without fault or provocation on the part of the plaintiff, been guilty of _____ [the grounds and the specific acts of misconduct are described].

That as a result of the defendant's acts of _____ of the kind described hereinabove, the plaintiff has become nervous and anguished, and has suffered _____ [the sleeplessness, hives, migraine headaches, ulcers, or whatever other symptoms are attributable to the unhappy marriage] and the differences between the plaintiff and the defendant are irreconcilable and the plaintiff has found living with the defendant to be intolerable and unendurable.

Now we get into the money:

That the plaintiff is not employed outside the home and is without means to support herself and the said minor children and to pay attorneys' fees and costs necessary to the conducting of this legal action; but that the defendant is able-bodied and is employed as _____ and earns a substantial salary in excess of $____ per week, and the defendant is well able to furnish suitable and sufficient support for the plaintiff and the said children and to pay attorneys' fees and costs of this action.

The complaint then prays the court to grant appropriate relief to the plaintiff:

WHEREFORE, the plaintiff, MARY SMITH, prays this Court as follows:

1. For a Decree of Divorce;

2. For such temporary and permanent alimony in installments or in gross, as the Court deems fit;

3. For temporary and permanent care, custody, control, and education of the two children of the marriage and for the temporary and permanent support of the said two children;

4. For temporary and permanent attorneys' fees in reasonable sums for the conduct of this litigation and for court costs and expenses of this litigation; and [here the plaintiff may also ask for injunctions, the deed to the house, a restoration of her maiden name, and so forth].

5. For such other and further relief as this Court may deem meet and equitable in the circumstances.

_____

MARY SMITH

The oath to a sworn complaint may look like this:

STATE OF _____   )
)   SS
COUNTY OF _____   )

MARY SMITH, being first duly sworn on her oath, deposes and states that she has read the above and foregoing Complaint for divorce by her subscribed and that the contents thereof are true.

_____

MARY SMITH

SUBSCRIBED AND SWORN TO
before me this ___
day of _____, 1973.

_____

Notary Public

If the complaint seems pompous, it's because it is bound up with centuries of legal tradition. If the complaint for divorce seems solemn, it is.

After the complaint is signed, the lawyer takes the complaint and the summons to the courthouse. The complaint is "filed" (at a cost of about $25.00). The clerk of the court stamps a number on the complaint and makes up a file. From that time on, the case is no longer your personal domestic problem, a little trouble in the family, or a rough spot "we'll work out." Now your "problem" is part of the public record and is known as *Smith* v. *Smith*, Circuit Court, No. 73 D 1234. The wheels of justice are officially set in motion. That same number is stamped on the summons and delivered to the sheriff, bailiff, or marshal and served on your husband who is now known, not as "that stinker," "that unfaithful worm," "that inconsiderate fool," but rather as the defendant in the matter of *Smith* v. *Smith*, Circuit Court, No. 73 D 1234.

Now the defendant, "him," hires a lawyer. Or if he doesn't want to contest the divorce, or the custody, or the support payments, or anything else, and if he doesn't want to pay a lawyer, he doesn't do anything. Assuming that he hires a lawyer to represent him, that lawyer will "file his appearance," the official notice to the court and to your lawyer that he is in the case. Then he will file his client's response to the complaint. This is usually called the "answer." Generally, the answer will admit that you were married and that the children were born of the marriage and deny everything else. Everything denied must be proven. Sometimes the defendant will file a countersuit for divorce claiming that it is he, not his wife, who has been wronged and that he should win the divorce suit. Almost always, as soon as the husband is served with the summons and a copy of the complaint, the barter over the property settlement begins.

From the moment the complaint is filed until the date the judge signs the decree, the case is pending. In his office, your lawyer is negotiating the property division; at home, you are reconsidering and re-reconsidering whether or not to go through with the divorce. All the while, legal procedures can be used as they are needed. For example, the wife's lawyer may seek temporary child support or attorneys' fees. The husband's lawyer may petition the court for an order giving the husband use of the car or rights to visit the children. If custody of the children is an issue, there may be a hearing to determine which parent should have custody until the case (and the final award of custody) is decided.

Don't be surprised if after all your battles and tears and after your firm resolve to divorce the man you've come to hate, the judge decides that your marriage can be saved. He can't order the two of you to live together, sup together, or sleep together, but he can order you to see a marriage counselor. Many states now have counseling services and many of those services have their offices right next door to the divorce court. In states that don't have their own counseling service, don't faint if the judge sends you to see a social worker, clergyman, or physician, or even if he calls husband and wife into his chambers for a chat. If the judge orders, or even if he only recommends, that you and your mate seek the advice of a third party—go. It's always a good idea to do as the judge says, but more than that, the intervention of a third party just may make a reconciliation possible. It's worth a try.

Injunctions and Discovery

A miserable scoundrel who likes nothing better than to take a swat at his wife rarely reforms when she files for divorce. Needless to say, some men turn meaner when the sheriff greets them with a summons and complaint. Once the case is filed, the court can do whatever is in its authority to protect a wife from her temperamental husband. For example, a court may order an injunction that tells someone to cease and desist from carrying on in some improper way. A "mandatory injunction" is a court order that demands that the person enjoined do some act directed by the judge. The woman who is in fear for her safety can ask the court for a temporary injunction to last while the suit is pending. The injunction can order the husband not to slug, beat, slap, or bruise the wife, not to telephone her, threaten her, harass or molest her, not to interfere with the children, and so forth. The man who warns his wife that he'll sell his property and hide the proceeds can be enjoined from selling anything without court approval. Men have even been enjoined from visiting their girl friends while their divorce case is pending.

Then there's the husband who tells you to go ahead and sue "but I won't move, I'll stay right here in the house." Do you have to cook his meals, iron his shirts, match his socks, trip over his beer bottles, golf clubs, and other belongings while your lawyer is battling his lawyer? And will he move out when the divorce is final? In most states, a lawyer can apply to the court for a mandatory injunction directing that our hero pack his bags and leave. It is not always the man who is ordered to move out. If there are children, however, the chances are that mother and children will get to remain in the house and dad will have to find a furnished room. The man who brags that he'll never pay alimony or child support because he is taking his cash and moving out of the state can be stopped by an order called a Writ of Ne Exeat. This writ orders the wanderer to put up a cash bond so that if he doesn't stay put until the divorce case is decided, the bond will supply the support.

If the sheriff knocks on the door and hands our hero an injunction, there is no guarantee that he'll follow it. In general, an order from the court carries just a bit more weight than all of your pleas, tantrums, and tears, and many men will be properly intimidated by the formal document. If he still carries on as before, your lawyer will prepare a Petition for a

Rule to Show Cause. This is a sworn statement, signed by the plaintiff, that the defendant is still up to his old tricks. A court date is set and if the judge believes that his order is being disobeyed, the sheriff will be on the scene again. This time the sheriff will pick up the violator of the injunction and escort him to the peace and comfort of the county jail.

Some men, particularly those men who suspect that divorce is in the wind, will go to great lengths to hide their money. Righteously, they argue that it is not that they don't want to support their dear little offspring, but that they don't think their wives should get a dime. These jewels rarely contest child custody, but are quite happy to turn their children over to these "nagging," "horrible," "ignorant" women. By secreting their assets, they obviously are keeping both their children and their children's mother without support. Thus, in order to uncover what the husband has so carefully covered, the wife's lawyer may use a variety of "discovery" procedures.

One method of discovery that is helpful in finding out where he has stashed the loot is the "discovery deposition." A deposition is a trial within a trial. In a deposition, the lawyer is allowed to cross-examine the witness (the husband, in this example). The deposition seems informal, especially since it is taken in a law office rather than a courtroom. But it's not the least bit casual, especially since a court reporter is sitting right there writing down every question and every answer, and the penalties of perjury apply. Should the circumstances require it, the wife's lawyer may subpoenae the depositions of business partners, employers, or others suspected of holding the defendant's cash.

Another discovery procedure is the direction to the husband to produce his books, records, tax returns, cancelled checks, and so forth. A physician who pocketed his patients' fees was ordered to produce his daily appointment calendar.

A real estate tycoon had to allow an appraiser to determine the value of his property, and another man's accounts were audited by the wife's accountant. And, because their wives were without the means to pay the expenses of their suits, these husbands were ordered to pay the bills of the appraiser and the accountant.

In the Courtroom

A contested divorce case is, to an attorney, just like any other civil trial. To the husband and wife involved, it is as bitter a confrontation as any courtroom battle between the state and the brutal ax murderer. There's no doubt that in any trial contest, the plaintiff and defendant must feel thoroughly frustrated. Trials are slow, the testimony is methodical, and it seems to take forever for your lawyer to finally get to the good stuff against your husband. The woman who is used to the speedy justice of an argument at the kitchen table and judgment by tossing the salad bowl in her husband's lap may find it difficult to understand why the whole proceeding takes so long and is so tedious. In fact, a contested divorce case may take two years to prepare and two days on trial. The trial only seems to go on forever.

A divorce case is an equity proceeding in an equity court. The plaintiff isn't asking for a money judgment, she is asking for a variety of kinds of relief, including a decree to dissolve the marriage, a determination of custody, and so forth. Traditionally, in Old English law, the King's Chancellor was charged with the duty of fashioning equitable relief. Today, in divorce cases, it is the equity judge who fashions the relief and *not* a jury. Many states stick with the old tradition and say a divorce case is an equity case, to be decided only by the equity judge, without a jury. Some states, though, have specifically said that a party in a divorce case may choose to have his case heard by a jury. Some states say that a jury may hear the evidence but only to advise the judge, not to bind him by their decision. A plaintiff in a state that allows a jury in divorce cases should not automatically decide that she'll demand a trial by jury. Depending on the facts that may come out in the trial, the judge, and the makeup of the jury, you may do better before a judge. This is a decision for the lawyer and his client to make together.

Husband and wife may hate each other thoroughly and both may fervently hope for a divorce. Yet, they may still square off and contest the property settlement. Husband and wife may agree to the divorce and alimony and, yet, they may go to court and contest child custody. So, it isn't necessary for a divorce contest to be between one spouse who wants a divorce and the other who wants to stay married. In fact, it hardly makes sense for a wife to contest her husband's desire for a divorce, go to court, fight to the mat, win the case, and then expect her husband to come home to dinner, a loving and faithful spouse.

A contested trial for divorce, custody, or alimony has everything that an X-rated movie can claim. It is expensive, emotional, a boon for gossips, and a trauma for children. This doesn't mean that the wife who has a valid reason to contest should surrender. It does mean that she should be sure the reason for a contest is good and valid.

The greatest percentage of divorces filed end up in uncontested trials. This may be because both parties want the divorce; she wants the kids and he wants only his camera and tripod; he has skipped town and doesn't show up in court; or because neither has the will, justification, or ready cash to contest the case.

No agreement between husband and wife, not even an agreement typed up, placed in a legal cover, sealed in wax, and bound with ribbon, can dissolve a marriage. Only the court has the power to decree a divorce. The uncontested case is still a court proceeding. The complaint is filed and generally, the property settlement agreement is worked out and signed. Then the husband lets the wife win by "default." A default in law is something like a forfeit in the Little League. If the opposing team doesn't show up, the team that's suited up and on the diamond gets an automatic win. In a default divorce case, the defendant doesn't answer the complaint, he files no appearance in court, or he agrees that even though he has filed an answer and his lawyer has filed an appearance, he will not show up to contest.

Even in a default divorce case, there may be some time spent before the decree is signed. After all, it took months of dating, courtship, wearing his letter sweater, class ring, fraternity pin, and engagement ring; having bridal showers; and choosing bridesmaids' dresses before you married. It should be at least as solemn, ceremonial, and time-consuming before you chuck it all. The law wants to give every couple every chance to stay married. The law wants to be sure that every defendant has a chance to be served with the summons, panic over the complaint, find himself a lawyer, and have his day in court. At a minimum then, a divorce won't be granted until twenty days after service of summons, and, in many states, no divorce case can be heard until at least ninety days after the sheriff hands over the summons. The spouse who has left the state before he is served has to have a chance to get the summons in the mail and return for the trial and if you've no idea where he's gone, the law will give him at least thirty days after you have filed suit and published a legal notice in a local newspaper announcing your intention to divorce him.

So, the first delay is to fulfill the legal requirement that the husband must have a chance to object. The next delay is the practical one because your lawyers are still nit-picking the property settlement agreement and because the judge's calendar is booked up. Marriage is so permanent and sacred these days that hundreds of divorce suits are filed every day. The judges assigned to divorce court are doing a land-office business. You simply have to wait your turn. But even in a big city, a simple uncontested divorce case can take as little as two to four months from filing to decree. Unless you're expecting your boyfriend's baby, that's hardly any time at all.

One day, when you are at the height of frustration and ready to fire your lawyer because you're sure he's been basking on a beach somewhere and ignoring his divorce client, a letter will come in the mail. It will be from that no-good shyster who will immediately rise from the ashes as the greatest counselor since Blackstone. The letter announces that your divorce case will be heard as a default on such and such a date.

The letter may tell you to show up with a witness or two. Now why do you need a witness when no one will be around to contest your right to win a divorce? Some state laws say that no default divorce may be granted without testimony of witnesses and this is required as a means of preventing collusive divorces. The law reasons that while a plaintiff may trump up grounds to get a divorce (and the defendant, who can't wait to run off with his secretary, may cheerfully allow his wife to testify to anything so that their marriage can be dissolved), an outsider may be unwilling to step up on the witness stand, swear to tell the whole truth, and then lie.

If your state is one that requires the testimony of witnesses at default divorce cases, look around. Best friends, neighbors, sisters, parents, and cousins (but keep your children out of it) are all prospects for you to call. Unless you have, in fact, dreamed up the grounds for divorce, you should find someone who is willing to testify and who can truthfully tell the judge how your husband gave you a black eye, that she saw the bruises, that he was rude to your friends, that you've lived alone for months, that the living room couch is made up as your bed, that he stays out late at night, that you're a terrific mother, and so forth. If no one will testify, it's a good bet that either the divorce case is collusive or your "friends" don't want to "get involved."

The judge hearing a default divorce case needs only to hear testimony to establish a *prima facie* divorce case. That is, he needs to be satisfied that the statements made in the complaint are true, and since your husband won't be in court to contest those statements, the judge is likely to accept your testimony. Once he agrees that the plaintiff and defendant were married, that the plaintiff was a faithful wife, and that the defendant committed grounds for divorce, he will order that the lawyer prepare a decree of divorce, he will sign the decree, and from that day on you're single again.

The default proceeding is simple. But there probably isn't a woman alive who won't suffer a touch of indigestion, a trembly voice, a tear, a pounding heart, or a clammy palm when she takes the witness stand. The whole thing takes fifteen minutes, but you'll swear you testified for hours.

Unless you've spent your life in a tree, you know what a courtroom looks like. It looks just like the courtrooms in the movies, the courtrooms on television, and the courtrooms in murder novels. Rows of spectator seats, counsel tables, witness stand, judge's bench, court reporter, clerk, bailiff, a flag, and a motto on the wall. The spectators watching the trial in the movies are cynical newspapermen, witnesses to the crime, the grieving family of the victim, and the gum-cracking, gun-toting girl friend of the accused. The spectators in divorce court are only other women and their witnesses waiting for their turn to step up and tell the judge their story. They aren't interested in you. You won't be interested in them. They'll watch you when it's your turn only because they are curious to know what will happen when their case is called. You'll listen to their cases, observe their lawyer's conduct, and check out what the other plaintiffs are wearing just to assure yourself that you are looking and acting as you should.

The testimony will sound something like this:

State your name.

State your address.

Are you the plaintiff in the suit of *Smith* v. *Smith*?

Are you presently married to John Smith?

When were you married?

Where were you married?

Have you lived in the City of _____, County of _____, State of _____, for one year immediately prior to the filing of the Complaint?

Were there any children born of this marriage?

Were any children adopted by you during the marriage?

Have you always conducted yourself as a good, faithful, and affectionate wife?

Have the children always resided with you?

Do you consider yourself a proper person to have the sole custody, control, and education of the children?

Do you consider your husband is not a fit person to have custody?

Calling your attention to _____, 1972, what, if anything happened between you and your husband?

Here is your chance to testify that he socked you, left you, stayed out all night, was sarcastic to your sister, called you names, and so forth. Then your lawyer will ask you questions to develop your testimony. For example, if you testify that he left you, the next question asks whether he returned, whether you caused or provoked his leaving you, whether he offered to return home, whether you have lived apart as single people (without sex) during the time of the desertion. If the grounds are mental cruelty, your lawyer will ask you to name other times when he treated you cruelly and the effect the cruelty had on you—sleeplessness, nervousness, weight loss, humiliation, and so forth.

Are you employed outside the home?

If there is a property settlement agreement, the lawyer will put it into evidence so that it becomes part of the decree.

I hand you a document, marked plaintiff's exhibit A for identification, which purports to be a Property Settlement Agreement entered into between you and your husband. Do you recognize it? Do you recognize the signatures on it?

After the agreement is identified, the lawyer will move that the agreement be admitted into evidence and if approved and if a decree is entered, that the agreement be made a part of the decree. The lawyer will then go through the high points of the agreement.

Does the agreement provide that the wife is to have custody, alimony of $_____ per month, and so forth?

When the lawyer has elicited enough testimony to prove that the plaintiff has made out her *prima facie* case, he excuses her. Knees wobbly, she steps down. The witnesses are called to testify to what they have observed while visiting the marital home.

The judge then will state whether or not you have won or lost, by telling the lawyer whether or not he may draft a decree to present for the judge's signature.

Off you go for coffee, a drink, a celebration, or a cry. But don't rush to the marriage license bureau to apply for husband number two. You aren't divorced yet!

The Decree

The decree is the court order that dissolves the bonds of matrimony. Until the judge signs the decree and the decree takes effect, plaintiff and defendant are still wife and husband. If the judge is convinced that the plaintiff has proven her case, he will order the plaintiff's lawyer to write up the decree for his signature.

The decree has four sections: the caption, the preface, the findings, and the order or decretal provisions. Again, it must be said that each lawyer has his own style for drafting a decree and each state has its own laws and court rules, but the decree for divorce may look like this:

[*The caption*]   )

STATE OF ———————)
) SS
)
COUNTY OF —————)
        IN THE CIRCUIT COURT OF —————COUNTY
                    EQUITY COURT

MARY SMITH,   )
)
            Plaintiff,   )
)
        v.   )   No. 73 D 1234
)
)
JOHN SMITH,   )
            Defendant.)

DECREE FOR DIVORCE

[*The preface*]

This cause coming on to be heard on the Complaint of MARY SMITH, the plaintiff, by her attorney, —————, and it appearing to the Court that defendant, JOHN SMITH, has had due notice of the pendency of this suit by personal service upon him of a Summons within this state and has failed to answer or appear, and an Order of Default having been entered against him;

And the Court having heard the testimony of witnesses taken in open court in support of said plaintiff's Complaint (a certificate of which evidence is filed herein)* and the Court now being fully advised in the premises, DOTH FIND:

[*The findings*]

1. That the Court has jurisdiction of the parties hereto and the subject matter hereof;

2. That the plaintiff is now and since, immediately prior to the filing of said Complaint, had been an actual resident of the City of _____, County of _____, State of _____, for more than one year;

3. That the plaintiff and defendant were lawfully joined in marriage on _____, 19 ___, at _____, _____;

4. That two children were born to the parties and none was adopted by them and said children are as follows:

Names   Birthdays

5. That the plaintiff at all times conducted herself as a true, faithful, and affectionate wife and is a fit and proper person to have the care, custody, control, and education of the said children of the parties;

6. That without fault or provocation of the plaintiff, the defendant has been guilty of _____ (grounds) as charged in the Complaint;

7. That the defendant is employed and receives a salary of $_____ per week and is well able to provide for plaintiff, and said children, and to pay the costs of this suit, but that the plaintiff is without funds or income to so provide; and

8. That the plaintiff and defendant have entered into a property settlement agreement dated _____, 19___, providing for the disposition and settlement of their respective rights,

---

* Attached to the decree is the court reporter's transcript of the trial in the case.

including provisions relative to alimony and child support, and that the Court finds that this agreement is fair, reasonable, and binding upon the plaintiff and defendant. A copy of the said property settlement was offered and admitted into evidence as plaintiff's Exhibit A and is attached hereto and by this reference made part of this decree for divorce.

[*The order or decretal provisions*]

On motion of _____, attorney for the plaintiff, MARY SMITH, it is hereby ORDERED, ADJUDGED, AND DECREED:

A. That the bonds of matrimony existing between MARY SMITH and JOHN SMITH be, and they are hereby dissolved;

B. That said property settlement agreement bearing the date of _____, 19__, is hereby incorporated into, merged within, and made a part of this decree for divorce and every provision is binding upon the parties; and

C. That this Court shall retain jurisdiction of this matter until the terms of this decree for divorce and the property settlement agreement incorporated herein have, in all respects, met full compliance.

ENTER:

_____
JUDGE

DATED: _____

In most states, the decree takes effect from the date the judge signs it, unless your state is one that has "interlocutory decree of divorce." Here's the state again stepping into the divorce proceeding and saying: "Hold it, slow down. This state considers your marriage a valuable status, worth saving. You'll have to wait before this divorce is final."

In the interlocutory decree states, a set amount of time must elapse. The judge signs the decree and it is called a decree *nisi*, a decree in the first place, but not a final decree. Then, after the judge signs, the interlocutory period starts; periods of, for example, three months in Utah, or six months in California. During the interlocutory period, the couple is legally married. Neither can remarry another, for to do so would be to commit bigamy.

A District of Columbia couple ended their marriage in bitter cross-complaints; she charging him with cruelty, he charging her with adultery (and naming a co-respondent). Both sought custody of their daughter. When the dust settled, the judge held him guilty of cruelty and her innocent of adultery and awarded child custody to the wife. The decree *nisi* was signed and the six-month interlocutory period began. After only a few days, the wife packed up her daughter and off she and the co-respondent went to a nearby state for a quick marriage, a bite to eat, and back home to D.C. When the first husband learned of the nuptials, he dashed into court and reported the week's events. The judge was furious. As long as the wife was domiciled in the Capitol she was subject to its laws and his jurisdiction. He declared her marriage bigamous and, reasoning that a woman who would commit bigamy is not a fit mother, awarded custody of the little girl to her father. Thus, an attempt to remarry during the interlocutory period is definitely forbidden, unless it is the plaintiff and defendant who decide to remarry each other. "Hooray," says the state, and the decree *nisi* is vacated and the couple remains married as soon as they make the request.

A Georgia woman was at her wit's end when she filed for divorce. She thoroughly hated her husband and was madly in love with her golf instructor. She counted the days until the thirty-day interlocutory period would end and her decree would become final. One day passed, then two, then two weeks, and suddenly she was in the courthouse with her lawyer applying for the vacation of the decree *nisi*. Did she have a change of heart? Did fickle fate turn her golf pro against her? Not at all. During the interlocutory period, her husband suddenly up and died. When the decree *nisi* was set aside, there was no question that she was an aggrieved widow—and also the beneficiary of the life insurance policies, the surviving spouse to the joint tenancy real estate and bank accounts, and the proud owner of several pairs of gold cuff links.

The decree *nisi* in an interlocutory decree state is then only another step closer to divorce and since both parties are husband and wife until the decree becomes final, they had better behave. If they sleep together during the interlocutory period, the winner of the decree has "condoned" the grounds of divorce committed by her spouse and he may move to set aside the decree *nisi*. If the winning party has an affair with her boyfriend, the loser may come into court, prove her guilty of adultery, and (because of the defense of "recrimination") have the decree *nisi* vacated.

The day the decree becomes final, the parties to a divorce are single and each can remarry. Except, that is, in a few states (Michigan, for example), which allow the judge to divorce the parties absolutely, but still provide in the decree that one of them (the "guilty" one) be prohibited from marrying again within a certain time period. If he does remarry in violation of the decree, he is in contempt of court and the newlyweds may have to set up housekeeping in jail. In Alabama, neither party to a divorce may remarry until after sixty days and if one of them appeals the divorce case, neither can remarry (except to each other) while the appeal is pending. If the plaintiff is just a wee bit pregnant with another man's child when she wins her Alabama decree, she may be a new mama before she can marry the baby's father.

When the decree becomes final, the court proceedings end, and so does the marriage. The decree, bound in a "blue back," the lawyer's cover, is yours to look at, fondle, and cherish. Then off it goes into the shoe box with your other valuable papers—your grade school graduation diploma, your membership certificate into the "Clean Plate Club," your Girl Scout merit award, and, of course, your marriage license.

26

Post-Decree—The Rest of Your Life

AND the judge handed down the decree, and the prince turned into a toad, and the princess drove off in a pumpkin-colored convertible, and everyone lived happily ever after.

If the marriage was a brief interlude and there were no children, chances are that this fairy tale can come true. Man and woman, once husband and wife, can, indeed, go their separate ways, take up their separate lives, and see their marriage fade in memory.

However, more often, even without considering the emotional trauma and the readjustment to single womanhood, the divorce decree ending a long-term marriage may signal not the end, but rather the beginning of a new round of legal dilemmas—not to mention emotional difficulties.

Interpreting the Property Settlement Agreement and Divorce Decree

Until every term of the divorce decree (and the property

settlement incorporated in it) is complied with, the divorce court's jurisdiction continues. Arguments over the meaning of particular clauses of the property settlement agreement may have to be decided by the judge after petitioning the divorce court. As a rule, though, disputes can and should be worked out between the former spouses and, if necessary, by the intervention of their lawyers.

When there are children, disagreements are all the more likely to arise. For example, let's assume that the property settlement provided that the mother is to pay the ordinary day-to-day medical and dental expenses, the father the extraordinary medical and dental expenses for the child. Clearly, mom is responsible for the semiannual checkups, vaccination, and orange-flavored aspirin tablets. Just as clearly, dad must pay for the treatment of beriberi, pellagra, and tic douloureux. But who pays when junior has a painful middle-ear infection, or sprains his wrist hanging from the parallel bars, or needs an afternoon a week with a child psychologist? Who pays for the ointments, salves, and other prescriptions? If baby's teeth come in on the bias, who pays the orthodontist to straighten them out?

Any one of these questions may be fought out by a battle royal in the post-decree division of the divorce court. But, hopefully, it may never come to that. In each case, start out by reading the decree in a manner most favorable to you: so long as your position is not ridiculous, try to get dad to pay. Where possible, let him know in advance that the medical bills are on their way. If that isn't practical, call him from the school nurse's office, emergency room, or dentist's reception room. Write him a polite note. But send on the bills! If he refuses to pay them, then there's plenty of time to decide whether you should call your lawyer or just dig down and pay the bills yourself.

The decree for divorce is a court order. For it to be changed, the party seeking the change must apply to the divorce court for permission to have the order modified. A court order is not a do-it-yourself kit for your former husband to tamper with to suit his convenience. From time to time he may—probably will—try and, unless you agree to the change, check with your lawyer to find out if it makes sense to go to court and keep your ex abiding with every detail of the order.

Former husbands can be very innovative in their interpretation of the divorce decree. For example, if the property settlement agreement provides for child support payable every single week and junior goes off to summer camp, don't be surprised if dad decides he doesn't have to pay child support for the summer. It is probably fair for you to agree with dad to take a reduction equal to your youngster's food budget when he's away, but only if dad is paying the full bill for summer camp. In other respects, junior's expenses continue whether he's home or living in a tent in the north woods. Landlords, for instance, have the peculiar habit of collecting rent even during July and August, and once his duffle bag is emptied out, and the missing socks, gym shoes, and bathing suits are inventoried, your son will be in line for a new school wardrobe.

Sometimes decrees set forth a flat weekly amount for child support rather than an individual weekly amount per child. The property settlement agreement may provide for child support of $60.00 per week rather than $20.00 for each of three children. If there is such a provision in your decree, you can count on dad to reduce his payments to $40.00 the very day that the oldest child reaches adulthood. Wait a minute. It may be that the decree contemplated payments of $60.00 per week as long as there is a child in the household. Or it may be that the eldest child's share of the $60.00 was less than one-third.

The rule is never to assume an interpretation of the decree that goes against you and your children's best interests. If *his* interpretation is not your interpretation, check with your lawyer. This is not to say that informal changes are absolutely forbidden. It is absurd to run to court over every nickel and dime. Furthermore, it may be that dad is willing to kick in a little extra now and then. Accept it graciously.

Modifying the Decree As to Payments

If the decree orders periodic payments of alimony and child support (or if the decree incorporates a property settlement agreement providing for these payments), then the divorce court is always available for either enforcement or modification of the terms. This means that so long as the woman is entitled to alimony (usually until she dies or remarries) and as long as the children are entitled to be supported by their father (usually until their majority), the divorce judge is waiting in the wings to offer his aid to see that the decree is performed and to see that the decree fits the present circumstances.

The first and most common post-decree "change" in the alimony and support payments is nonpayment. As time goes on, some men conveniently "forget" the agreement they signed and the judge's order. This is particularly the case when a man, once again facing the world as a bachelor, takes on a variety of new responsibilities, such as the responsibility to furnish his apartment with model boats, bar glasses that say "Name Your Own Poison," Bardot posters, a man-made fake-fur bedspread, and a variety of antique rifles, swords, and chains.

Once our hero has acquired a newly slimmed-down waistline, a bouffant toupee, and a suede wardrobe, he actually may succeed in finding the woman of his dreams. Yet, even if he does remarry, a man cannot ignore his obligations of alimony and support. Remarriage is a voluntary act. When a man decides to marry again, he should make the initial decision of whether he can support a new marriage while still dispensing his legal obligations. If he can't, he shouldn't.

Remarriage, even a remarriage carrying with it the new wife's "old" children, or the start of a second family, rarely, if ever, relieves a man from the duty to support his first family.

Even the man who declares bankruptcy is not excused from his duty of support. Unless illness totally disables him and he finds himself on the welfare rolls, the requirements of the divorce decree still exist.

The man who thinks he has a valid reason not to pay or to pay less cannot "take the law into his own hands." The decision is not his to make. He must apply to the court to seek a modification of the decree. After both sides have an opportunity to present their case, it is up to the judge to decide whether the man has given sufficient reason so that the judge can lower the ante.

Modifications of the divorce decree may be allowed only if there is a substantial change in circumstances. Modifications may be sought by either the former husband or wife and payments may be increased, decreased, or left the same. The only issue before the court on modification is change in circumstances—not the guilt or innocence of the parties in the earlier divorce case. One of the most convincing reasons for post-decree change of alimony and support payments is the fact that everything else has changed while the amount of the payments has not.

For example, a man divorces his wife leaving her with custody of two preschoolers and $50.00 a week for their support. Years pass. The cost of living is up. The "preschoolers" now eat lunch in a school cafeteria, go to movies, birthday parties, and Scout overnights. One wears $25.00-a-pair correctional orthopedic oxfords, and the other longs for toe shoes. Mother has taken a part-time job but, even so, they can barely manage. Meanwhile, father has had two job promotions, one new title, a half-dozen salary increases, and a three-week paid vacation. This woman can show a substantial change in circumstances while the support payments have remained static, and she well may succeed in obtaining a modification in the decree increasing the weekly stipend.

The man may also come to court and claim a change in circumstances such that the payments should be *decreased*. His burden will not be lightened merely because of his voluntary acts. That is, he cannot relieve himself of his job and claim hardship. He cannot complain because of his burdensome new car payments. Nor will his remarriage to a demanding young wife alleviate his duties. There are circumstances, though, on which he may rely for a reduction in payments, such as illness or involuntary unemployment. When a Florida couple divorced, Mrs. L was a housewife without income and Mr. L was a highly successful attorney. After the decree, Mrs. L completed her education and became a teacher, while Mr. L, despite his best efforts, saw his practice reduced to only a few clients who rarely paid their bills. He succeeded in obtaining a reduction in alimony.

One of the significant changes that may relieve a man of his duty to continue the initial alimony payments is a woman's new-found wealth. This does *not* mean that the woman who receives alimony should refuse to work for fear of losing it. As stated by the high court of Arizona, "the mere fact that the wife has secured employment since the entry of the decree for alimony is not within itself a grounds for modification. It is but a circumstance to be considered. . . ." That Arizona court refused to reduce alimony when the only reason given was the woman's being employed. If the law were otherwise, a woman would be penalized (and a man rewarded) if she found a job. A divorced woman would have little incentive to join (or rejoin) the labor market. In addition, courts, in looking at the earnings of working mothers, consider not only their salaries, but their expenses in holding down a job outside the home.

While a change in circumstances may increase or decrease the child support payments, it is a universal truth that a father cannot assign away his duty to provide some support for his children. On a woman's remarriage, she will lose her right to *alimony*, but the duty to support the children remains with their father, not with their mother's new husband. Grandparents have been known to make gifts to help out in the support of their grandchildren; their gifts, though, are entirely voluntary. A Colorado man claimed that he should be relieved of any duty of support of his children because his wife's parents generously contributed to their support. The judge pointed out that it is the father's duty to provide for his offspring, and he must continue to do so no matter how generous others might choose to be.

Collecting Unpaid Alimony and Support

One of life's sweet moments comes when the postman arrives. After sorting through the occupant mail, the divorced woman brightens at seeing the envelope from her former spouse containing his weekly love note beginning "Pay to the order of. . . ." When the mail stops carrying his check and your calls and notes go unanswered, it's off to the lawyer.

Because nonpayment is a violation of the court order, the wife's lawyer may serve "A Petition for a Rule to Show Cause" why the man should not be held in contempt of court. It is then the former husband's job to come to court and explain to the judge why his gambling junket to Las Vegas was more compelling than his duty of child support. The man who willfully ignores a court order that has necessitated getting his wife legal assistance may be directed to pay her attorney's fees and court costs for the post-decree proceedings. If he is held in contempt of court, the errant spouse may be sent to jail.

For a woman who has been wronged, seeing her ex go to

jail may produce a warm glow of satisfaction, but that warm glow won't put dinner on the table. While the threat of a jail term may keep a man paying, it won't, in itself, provide for collection of the únpaid money. Furthermore, to send a man to jail for contempt, he first must be caught. Some men grab the decree and skip out of state. Other men fall behind in their payments and then do the ultimate act to avoid the law, they die.

Beyond the judge's lecture, the possibility of thirty days in jail, or the chance of losing visitation rights, there must be some way to collect the past-due money from these men so that the rent may be paid and the children cared for. There is. If a man has some money or property, or if he is earning a salary and is behind in his alimony and support payments, the former wife can choose her method. She may apply to the judge for a contempt order, or she may go to court and file a separate lawsuit against him to reduce the unpaid balance to a judgment. She will win her judgment if she can prove that he has not paid her as ordered. She may then seek to collect the amount of the judgment.

Depending upon the various states' laws, a judgment may be collected in any number of ways. For example, the judgment may be made a "lien" on the debtor's property. A lien is a notice that tells potential buyers that someone has a claim to be paid from the proceeds of a sale and that the title will not be clear unless the lien-holder is paid off. On a sale of the property, the lien-holder gets a share of the purchase price equal to the value of the lien (the amount of the judgment). On payment, the lien is removed.

Another means of collecting a judgment is bit-by-bit from the debtor's wages. This is called a garnishment. A garnishment is a three-way means of collecting. It goes like this. Acme Trucking owes Mr. J his salary every week. Mrs. J has a judgment for unpaid alimony and starts a garnishment proceeding against Acme. The garnishment court orders

Acme to pay Mrs. J a certain percent of Mr. J's salary every week until her judgment is paid off.

There may be half a dozen ways to collect a judgment in your state, but none of them works against a man who has no money and no job. And the wife who gets a judgment must rely on it. If the judgment goes unpaid, she cannot go back to divorce court and ask that her husband be jailed for not paying the amount of the judgment. According to the Constitution, a person may be jailed for contempt of court, but not for nonpayment of a judgment debt. It's a fine line, but debtors' prisons belong in Charles Dickens' novels, not in American jurisprudence.

The man who has the nerve to die owing alimony and support may leave an estate. A claim for past-due alimony and support is a proper claim against a probate estate. But no matter how large the estate, the obligation to pay alimony and support dies with the spouse, and a father also may disinherit his children. The only allowable probate claim then is for unpaid payments that were due prior to the time of his death.

In order to collect past-due payments, the woman must *find* her former husband. There was a time when a man could avoid his obligations simply by packing up and leaving the state. A *final* judgment rendered in one state was valid in every other state because of the "full faith and credit" clause of the Constitution. But an order for alimony or support is always subject to modification as circumstances change. Thus the judiciary at one time held that while the part of the decree divorcing parties was valid everywhere, the support portion of the orders was not *final*. The "full faith and credit" clause did not apply to support orders. So even if the woman knew where her husband could be found, she could collect only by starting all over again in her former husband's new home state. She had to prove again that she was entitled to alimony and child support and that the amounts set forth in the original order were proper. Only then could she collect for any unpaid amounts.

If a woman spent a year fighting out a divorce suit in New York and proved that she was entitled to alimony in a monthly amount, that order was valid only in New York and was meaningless everywhere else. The husband who didn't like the alimony award rendered in New York could go to Illinois and start the trial all over again, and if he thought the alimony award was too high in Illinois, he could choose another state to settle in.

Out of this chaos was born "The Uniform Reciprocal Enforcement of Support Act," which has now been enacted into law in more than half of the states. Under the uniform act, a woman with a decree in one state can enforce it in the other states. Those "other" states will accept the order as is. It will be honored in every state as if those states had entered the order in the first place. The husband can alter the order only by seeking a modification because of a change in circumstances. Thus, the original support order may be modified, but not abandoned.

The woman whose husband skips the state owing support sees her lawyer in her home state. Her lawyer then arranges to have the decree and arrearage brought to the attention of the courts of the state where the errant spouse is hiding. Those courts will enforce the decree just as if they had made it.

Changes in Visitation

A significant and obvious change that occurs in the years following the decree for divorce is that the babies grow up. The toddler who docilely went off with dad every Sunday suddenly becomes a preteen who has his own Sunday plans. The decree that provides for visitation on a definite schedule worked out between mom and dad becomes a weekly chore to a kid with a mind and social life of his or her own. Normally, the father will not insist that his son stare at him all Sunday when he'd rather be at the high school football field.

Changes in visitation can and should be worked out to accommodate the schedules of the parents and their children. The child who goes to camp for the summer won't be around to see his dad every weekend. The woman who saves up to take her kids on a European vacation will be denying dad some visiting days. She should arrange to let him make up those days later.

A father has little reason to deny his children the benefits of camping and travel because he may miss one or two Sunday visits, but mom should be flexible, too. She should agree to dad's taking the offspring to the theater, out to dinner, or on a weekend vacation, and he and the near-adult children should work out schedules to suit all of them. This does *not* mean that children should be encouraged to ignore their visiting father. It must be remembered that the law considers visitation to be a benefit to the children, not just a salve to the noncustodial parent.

The woman whose decree grants visitation to her ex cannot defeat his rights of visitation. If the father skips his child support payment, the mother must go to court to have him ordered to pay up. She should *not* simply decide for herself that he has forfeited his right to see the children. He has a court-granted right to visitation and only the court can take it away.

Similarly, a woman cannot, in effect, defeat the right of visitation by moving so far away that the husband cannot see the children without boarding a jet. If she wishes to pack up and leave the court's jurisdiction (and, therefore, leave dad miles from the children), she must ask the court's permission. She must petition the court, explaining the reasons for the move, hopefully agreeing to the children's weekend visits or their taking vacation trips with dad, and ask the judge for permission to leave town.

If the children you have nurtured and protected come in on Sunday evening with a glowing description of the inside of a neighborhood tavern, a new vocabulary of four-letter words, a hair-raising account of what it's like to play in the traffic, or a peaceful report of how they watched TV while daddy kissed the blonde lady, it's time for parents to have a chat. Fathers have lost their visitation rights when they have abused them, and, if the chat does not result in better behavior, it may be time to apply to the court for a limitation of the rights of visitation.

But on the other hand, after a weekend at the seashore with their father, the children are quite likely to come home with chills, stomach cramps, and athlete's foot. Dad may keep them up past their bedtime and fill them with pepperoni pizza and pastrami sandwiches. You may spend the entire week after their return nursing them back to health so that dad can do the whole thing all over again next Sunday. In such cases, it's again time for a parental chat, but understand that a judge will sympathize with a father whose intentions are good, but whose babysitting is inept.

Changes in Custody

So long as the children are minors, the court may order a change in custody. There is no such thing as a final award of custody. Once custody is determined in the decree, though, the children adjust to living with the custodial parent—they are enrolled in school; they make friends in the neighborhood; and so forth. The courts are reluctant to bounce a child from parent to parent upsetting all of these relationships. In order to effect a change in custody, the judge must be convinced that the best interests of the child demand that the change be made. As the child matures, he or she may request a change in custody. While the courts will not (and cannot, as a practical matter) ignore the wishes of a near-adult, they will not change custody, even in this situation, unless they are convinced that the best interests of the child will be served.

When his former wife was stricken with diabetes and recurring hepatitis, a Georgia man maintained that she was unable to care for the children and urged that custody be switched to him. The court refused him his request, finding that the children were well cared for and that the illness was not a significant enough change in circumstances. When Mr. M won his divorce from the woman who deserted him and the children, he also won custody. He was a rigid man who spanked his kids for talking in church, spanked them for splashing the bath water, spanked them for leaving their dinner unfinished, and spanked them, and spanked them, and spanked them. But the judge said that while Mr. M was undoubtedly a strict disciplinarian, he was neither unmerciful nor brutal, and custody was not changed.

Because a change in custody greatly upsets a child's routine, the courts will rarely direct a change because of a parent's occasional moral lapse. The parent who has had custody must clearly abuse the privilege of child custody before the court will change it. Even if Mr. J had proven that his wife had committed adultery with the man who became her second husband, the Supreme Court of Hawaii held that she had always cared for the children and that now that she was remarried, the home was a fit one in which to rear them.

Thus, the custodial parent's remarriage, in itself, is not a change in circumstances to warrant a change in custody. In fact, if the custodial parent remarries, the home may prove even more stable and thus provide a better atmosphere for bringing up the child. But the woman who has custody and wants to keep it had better choose her second husband (and her children's stepfather) carefully. One woman lost custody of the children of her first marriage when she married for the second time, divorced, and married for the third time, all within a few years; both remarriages were to men with criminal records. The judge interviewed the children in chambers and was aghast to find that the eight-year-old boy rarely attended school, but had a vocabulary well-spiced with swear words and could describe in detail how he put his drunken stepdad to bed every night.

Mrs. A lost custody of her two daughters when the neighbors testified to a number of questionable incidents, including the time the stepfather was seen in an alleyway next to a hotel carrying one of the girls in his arms and fondling her breast. The judge's decision to change the girls' custody was simplified, too, because their father had remarried to a woman who was well suited to provide them with an orderly and loving home life.

Since the divorce decree fixing custody is a court order, the person who wants custody changed must apply to the court. The parent who "changes" custody simply by taking the child and skipping town is kidnapping the child. States generally decide not to prosecute and punish such parents for kidnapping, but prosecutions for such acts occasionally do occur. Even more importantly, "taking" the child is self-defeating. The judge may decide that the parent who would steal away with a child in violation of his order will never qualify as a fit and proper parent.

Apart from the divorce court, there are two ways that child custody may be changed. The first way is by an adoption proceeding. Mom remarries and her new husband wants to adopt her children as his own. The adoption means that the natural father need not support his children and does not have a right to visit with them. The adopting father has all of the rights and obligations as if he were the children's natural father. The new husband may adopt only if the father gives his written consent or if he has so grossly neglected his children that the adoption judge decides that he has lost the right to them. Adoption is a court proceeding and until the adoption takes place, the mother has no right to change the child's last name to that of her new spouse.

The second way custody is changed without applying to the divorce court is on the death of the custodial parent. Ordinarily, upon the death of the custodial parent, child custody passes automatically to the surviving parent. For the woman who has divorced a man after he neglected or abused his children, this is a chilling thought. Such a woman should return to her lawyer's office and have a will drawn. In her will she should designate a guardian of her choice for the children and trust that, should she die while the children are minors, the guardian will make every legal effort to prevent custody from passing automatically to the errant father.

* * *

And so the judge handed down the decree, and the decree was from time to time modified, and the decree was enforced, and everyone lived happily ever after.

Grounds for Divorce Recognized in Each State*

	Alabama	Alaska	Arizona	Arkansas	California	Colorado	Connecticut	Delaware	District of Columbia	Florida	Georgia	Hawaii	Idaho	Illinois	Indiana	Iowa	Kansas	Kentucky	Louisiana	Maine	Maryland
Abandonment	●	●	●	●			●	●	●		●	●	●	●	●		●	●	●	●	●
Adultery	●	●	●	●			●	●	●		●	●	●	●	●		●	●	●	●	●
Attempted Murder														●							
Bigamy				●				●						●							●
Drug Addiction		●										●	●							●	
Drunkenness	●	●	●	●			●	●			●	●	●	●	●		●	●		●	
Fraud								●			●			●				●			
Impotency	●	●	●	●							●				●			●		●	●
Imprisonment (felony conviction)	●	●	●	●			●	●	●		●	●		●	●		●	●	●		●
Incest											●										●
Incompatibility	●	●						●									●				
Insanity	●	●		●	●		●	●		●	●	●		●			●	●			
Mental Cruelty		●	●				●	●			●	●	●	●	●		●	●		●	●
Neglect of Duty (Nonsupport)		●	●	●				●				●	●		●		●	●		●	
No-fault	●				●	●		●		●						●					
Non-age								●													●
Physical Cruelty		●	●	●			●	●			●	●	●	●	●		●	●		●	
Pregnancy (by another)	●	●									●							●			
Religion Forbidding Sex																		●			
Sodomy (and buggery)	●																				
Unexplained Absence (Enoch Arden)							●														
Venereal Disease													●					●			
Voluntary Separation	●		●	●			●	●			●	●						●	●		●

216

Column headers (left to right):

Missouri · Montana · Nebraska · Nevada · New Hampshire · New Jersey · New Mexico · New York · North Carolina · North Dakota · Ohio · Oklahoma · Oregon · Pennsylvania · Puerto Rico · Rhode Island · South Carolina · South Dakota · Tennessee · Texas · Utah · Vermont · Virgin Islands · Virginia · Washington · West Virginia · Wisconsin · Wyoming

217

Index

A

Abandoned children, 120
Abandonment: *see* Desertion
Adoption
    child support, 131
    custody, change of, 214, 215
    unfit parents, 121
Adultery
    adulteress, consequences, 35
    alimony, denial of, 140
    child custody, 120, 121
    child support allowance, 131
    condonation, 80, 81
    confessions in court, 86
    connivance, 91, 92
    co-respondents, 33-35
    definitions, past and
        present, 25-27

    interlocutory period, 200
    limitations, statute of, 77
    mental cruelty, 57, 58
    proof of, 27-32
    recrimination defense, 88, 89
Advocacy, 95
Alcoholism, 42, 43, 92, 120
Alienation of affections, 33
Alimony
    amount, 141-145
    complaint, document of, 183,
        184
    court jurisdiction, 105-108,
        163
    denial of, 139-141
    income tax, 151-153
    modification, 204-206
    no-fault divorce, 73
    nonpayment, 207-210

payment, terms of, 145-149
settlement sample, 170-173
temporary, 148
waiving of, 139, 171
Animals, intercourse with, 27, 54
Annulment, 4-8
"Answer," 185
Antenuptial agreements, 160, 161
Appeal, 100
Assault: *see* Physical cruelty
Assets, disclosure of, 162, 170, 188, 189

B

Bank account ownership, 164-166, 176
Bankruptcy, 205
Bar association, 96
Bigamy, 5, 114
Blackmail, 34
Breach of contract, 163
Buggery, 27, 54

C

Car, 176
Children
adoption, 121, 131, 214, 215
complaint, document sample, 183
court jurisdiction, 105-108
court testimony, 31
custody, 116-123
custody changes, 127, 212-215
"dependent," defined, 153-156
legitimacy, 130, 131
no-fault divorce, 72, 73
parents, legal duties of, 9, 130
settlement rights, sample, 172-175, 177
visitation changes, 210-212
visitation rights, 124-128
Children, support allowance
adopted, 131
amount, 132-134
college education, 137
complaint, document of, 183, 184
disabled, 136
duration, 136, 137
former marriage, 131
income tax, 153-156
nonpayment, 207-210
payment, terms of, 130-132, 134-136
settlement modification, 202-207
settlement sample, 172-175
College education, support money for, 137
Collusion, 83-86
adultery admissions, 30, 31
witnesses required, 192
Comity, 113
Common law, English, 118, 119
Common-law marriage, 2, 3
Community property, 145, 168
Comparative rectitude, 90

Complaint, 180-186
Condonation, 79-83
  complaint, document of,
    182
  interlocutory period, 200
Conjugal rights, 56
Connivance, 90-92
Consortium, 33
Constructive desertion, 23
Contested divorce, 189, 190
  child custody, 118
  threat of, 75
  validity in other states, 111
Contingent fee, 98
Contract, breach of, 163
Co-Respondent, 33-35
Costs of suit, 99, 100
Counseling services, 186
Countersuit for divorce, 185
Court
  complaint, filing the, 180-186
  contempt of court, 163, 209
  _____ of equity, 87, 104
  injunctions, 186-188
  reporter's fee, 99
  settlement, modification or
    enforcement, 204-207
Court jurisdiction, 75, 103-108
  complaint, sample, 182
  divorce decree sample, 198
  moving away, 211
  post-decree, 202, 204
  property settlement, 161,
    163, 164
  visitation changes, 126, 127
Criminal conviction
  connivance, 92
  desertion grounds, 16

  divorce grounds, 36-38
  recrimination defense, 88
Cruelty: *see* Physical cruelty;
    Mental cruelty
Cunnilingus, 26, 64
Custody: *see* Children

D

Death
  custody, change in, 215
  presumption of, 67
  probate claim after, 209
Debts, responsibilities for, 10,
    176
Decree, divorce: *see* Divorce
Decree *nisi*, 198-200
Default divorce, 68, 191-193
Deposition, 188
Desertion
  court jurisdiction, 107, 108
  disappearance, 67
  justification for, 22-24
  legal qualifications, 15
  relationship defined, 20-22
  time requirement, 18-20
  voluntary or unintentional,
    16-18
Detectives, use of, 31, 32
Disabled offspring, support,
    136
Disappearance of spouse: *see*
    Desertion
Discovery procedures, 188, 189
Disinheriting children, 177
Dividends, stock, 168

Divorce
  contested, 75, 118, 189, 190
  cost of, 97-101
  countersuit, 185
  court jurisdiction, 104-108
  decree, 159, 163, 178, 196-
    200, 202-207
  default, 68, 191-193
  defenses to, 74-92
  " _____ from bed and
    board," 11
  foreign, validity, 113, 114
  grounds by state, chart, 216,
    217
  no-fault statute, 71-73
  pressured into, 84
  "quicky" divorce, 109-115
  state laws and power, 12-14
  uncontested, 190, 192
  validity in other states, 111
  voluntary separation, 69
Domicile, 109-112
  choice of, 17
  foreign country, 113
Drug addiction, 43, 44, 120
Drunkenness, 42, 43, 92, 120
Due process, 105
Duty, neglect of, 39-41

Enoch Arden laws, 67
Equity court, 87, 104, 189
Estate, probate claim, 209
Exemptions, tax, 153-156

F

Fees, lawyer, 97-101
Fellatio, 26, 64
Felony, 37, 38, 88
Filing the case, fee for, 99, 185
Financial support: *see* Alimony;
  Children, support allow-
  ance; Property settlement;
  Support
Flat fee, 99
Foreign divorce, 114
Forgiveness, defense of, 79-83
Fraud
  annulment grounds, 7
  involuntary divorce, 85
Full disclosure of assets, 162,
  170
"Full faith and credit clause,"
  109-113, 209
Furniture, 176

E

Emancipation, child support
  after, 136
Emotional illness, 51
Employment, alimony during,
  206

G

Garnishment, 208, 209
Grounds for divorce, chart,
  216, 217
Guardian, 215
Guardian Ad Litem, 51

Guilt, 72, 90-92

H

Habits, disgusting, 56
Handicapped children, support of, 136
Health
   complaint, document of, 183
   danger to, 54, 55, 60, 64
   expenses, payment of, 176, 177
Homosexuality, 57
Hourly rate, 98, 99

I

Impotency, 45-49
   annulment, grounds for, 7
   child support allowance, 131
   condonation, 80
   limitations, statutes of, 78
Incest, 5
Income, definition, 172
Income tax
   agreement, sample, 175
   alimony, 151-153
   alimony in gross, 146
   child support, 153-156
   joint return, 150, 151
   legal fees, 156, 157
Incompatibility, 72
Inheritance agreements, 160, 161
Injunctions, 186-188
   against harassment, 24, 187

assets, freezing of, 142
complaint, document of, 184
forbidding return of spouse, 24
paramour, 33, 34
In-laws, 17, 18, 125
In personam jurisdiction, 105-108, 112, 113
In rem jurisdiction, 108, 112, 113
Insanity, 50-52
Insurance beneficiaries, 177
Intercourse: *see* Sexual intercourse
Interlocutory decree of divorce, 198-200
Interracial marriage, 5
Irreconcilable differences, 71

J

Jailed spouse
   connivance, 92
   contempt of court, 209
   desertion grounds, 16
   divorce grounds, 36-38
Joint tenancy, 165, 166, 176
Judge, responsibilities of, 159
Judgment, 208, 209
Jurisdiction: *see* Court jurisdiction
Jury, divorce trial by, 189, 190

K

Kidnapping, 214

L

Laches, 76, 78
Lawsuits
  breach of contract, 163
  cost of, 99, 100
  release from, 178
  support nonpayment, 208
Lawyers
  defendant, 185
  finding, 93-97
  income taxes, 156, 157
  payment, post-decree, 207
  payment of, 97-101, 178
  right to have, 170
  treatment of, 101, 102
Legitimacy, 130, 131
Lien, 208
Limitations, Statutes of, 75-78
Locking spouse out, 23, 24
"Long-arm" jurisdiction, 106

M

Mail-order foreign divorce, 114
Maintenance, separate, 10, 11,
  154, 155
"Majority," 136
Mandatory injunction, 187
Marriage, legal status, 2-8
Marriage counselor, 186
Masturbation, 48, 56
Medical expenses: *see* Health
Mental cruelty, 53-58
  no-fault, 72
  statutes of limitations, 78

  testimony, 194, 195
Mental institution, 51
Miscegenation, 5
Misdemeanor, 37, 38
Mistress, 33-35
Money, complaints about
  spending, 55
Mother, unfit, 119, 120
Moving, choice of, 17, 127, 211
Multiple support agreement,
  156

N

Name-calling, 55
Neglect of children, 120, 121
Neglect of duty, 39-41
Nevada divorce, 109-112
No-fault divorce, 71-73
  community property, 145
  voluntary separation, 69

O

Overtime salary, 175
Ownership, proof of, 164-168

P

Paramour, 33-35
Parents, duties of, 9, 130
Parents, living with, 17, 18

Answer

Paternity suit, 30
Perjury
  collusion, 84
  deposition, 188
  pleading, 181
Personal habits, 56
Petition for a Rule to Show
    Cause, 187, 188, 207
Physical cruelty, 59-65
  condonation, involuntary,
    81
  mental cruelty, 55
  recrimination defense, 88
Plaintiff, 180
Pleading, divorce, 181
Polygamy, 5
Postnuptial agreements, 160,
    161
Pregnancy
  annulment, grounds for, 7
  bride's fraud, 79, 80
  decree finalized, 200
  premarriage, child support,
    131
Prima facie case, 181, 193, 195
Private eye, use of, 31, 32
Probate estate, claim against,
    209
Property
  court jurisdiction, 105-108
  disappearance of spouse, 67
  ownership, 164-168
  settlement, sample, 176
Property settlement, 158-160
  child support, 130, 134, 136,
    137
  contents, 164-168
  contents, sample, 169-179

decree, incorporating into,
    163, 164, 178, 179
  modification of, 202-207
  moving plans, 127
  negotiation, 160, 161
  tax deductions, 156
  testimony, 195
  validity, 161, 162
  visitation rights, 125
  see also Alimony; Children,
    support allowance
Protection of wife, 55

Q

Quicky divorces, 109-115

R

Races, marriage between, 5
Real estate: *see* Property
Reconciliation
  condonation defense, 82, 83
  counseling, 186
  desertion, 20
  foreclosure, 34
  lawyer's fee, 97
Recrimination, 87-90
Rectitude, comparative, 90
Religion, choice of, 56, 120
Remarriage
  alimony, terms of, 146
  custody changes, 213, 214
  interlocutory period, 199

post-decree, 200
support obligations continue, 204-207
Residence: *see* Domicile
Residence requirements, 108, 109
Residences, separate, 21, 22
Retainer system, 97

S

Self-defense, 62
Separate maintenance, 10, 11
  desertion, 19, 20
  tax exemptions, 154, 155
Separation
  death, presumption of, 67
  desertion, 21, 22
  "_____ from bed and board," 21
  voluntary, 68-70
Sexual conduct, deviate, 26, 27, 54
Sexual intercourse
  abnormal, 64
  adultery defined, 26
  complaint document, 182
  condonation, 78-83
  conjugal right, 56, 57
  desertion timetable, 21
  excessive demands, 63, 64
  impotency, 45-49
  interlocutory period, 200
  marriage validity, 8
  voluntary separation grounds, 70

Silent treatment, 55
Sodomy, 27
Split custody, 119
State
  court jurisdiction, 105-108
  divorce, role in, 12, 13
  divorce validity, 109-112
  support validity, 210
  see also Court jurisdiction
Stocks, ownership of, 165, 168
Summons
  court jurisdiction, 105, 106
  fee, 99
  serving of, 185
  time following notification, 191
Support
  child, 129-137
  desertion defined, 21
  neglect within marriage, 39-41
  see also Alimony; Children, support allowance

T

Taxes: *see* Income Tax
Temporary injunction, 187
"Tenancy by the entirety," 166, 167
"Tenancy in common," 167
Testimony
  children, 31
  collusion, 84
  court reporter's fee, 99, 100
  default proceeding, 193-195

detectives, 32
doctors, 49
former wife, 48
lawyers, 102
voluntary admissions, 30
witnesses, 192
Threats
marriage under, 6
mental cruelty, 55
property settlements, 162
Titles of ownership, 164-168
Transcript, 99, 197
Transferee, need to follow, 17
Trust, establishment of, 177

Uniform Reciprocal Enforcement of Support Act, 210

V

Venereal disease, 63
Violence: *see* Physical cruelty
Visitation, 124-128
changes in, 210-212
property settlement, 173,
174
Voidable marriages, 5-8
Voluntary separation, 69

U

Uncontested divorce, 190, 192
Underage marriage, 6
Unfit mother, 119, 120

W

Wages, garnishment of, 208
Witnesses, 86, 192
Writ of Ne Exeat, 187